GAME-CHANGING LIFE SKILLS FOR TEENS

Navigating Adulthood with Confidence: The Ultimate Guide to Overcome Challenges, Build Meaningful Relationships, Manage Money, and Much More.

ANGELA ABRAHAM

ataraxio
BALANCE, GROW, EXCEL

© **Copyright 2024 - All rights reserved.**

The content contained within this book may not be reproduced, duplicated or transmitted without direct written permission from the author or the publisher.

Under no circumstances will any blame or legal responsibility be held against the publisher, or author, for any damages, reparation, or monetary loss due to the information contained within this book, either directly or indirectly.

Legal Notice:

This book is copyright protected. It is only for personal use. You cannot amend, distribute, sell, use, quote or paraphrase any part, or the content within this book, without the consent of the author or publisher.

Disclaimer Notice:

Please note the information contained in this document is provided for educational and entertainment purposes only. It should not be considered professional advice in any field, including but not limited to medical, financial, legal, or psychological matters. The author is not a licensed therapist, doctor, financial advisor, or practicing professional in these fields. The content within this book has been derived from various sources. Please consult a licensed professional before attempting any techniques outlined in this book.

This book contains general advice and suggestions based on research and personal experience. However, every individual's situation is unique. Before making any significant decisions or changes related to your health, finances, or personal life, it's strongly recommended that you consult with appropriate licensed professionals.

The content in this book is not intended to be a substitute for professional medical advice, diagnosis, or treatment. Always seek the advice of your physician or other qualified health provider with any questions you may have regarding a medical condition.

Regarding financial information, this book is for educational and entertainment purposes only. You should not construe any information or other material as legal, tax, investment, financial, or other professional advice. Nothing in this book constitutes a recommendation to buy or sell securities or make investment decisions. You are solely responsible for your own financial decisions.

All effort has been executed to present accurate, up to date, reliable, complete information. No warranties of any kind are declared or implied. However, they make no representations or warranties of any kind, express or implied, about the completeness, accuracy, reliability, suitability, or availability of this book's information, products, services, or related graphics.

Therefore, any reliance on such information is strictly at your own risk. In no event will the author or publisher be liable for any loss or damage, including, without limitation, indirect or consequential loss or damage, or any loss or damage whatsoever arising from loss of data or profits arising out of, or in connection with, the use of this book.

Remember, the key to success is to take action, learn from your experiences, and adapt as needed. Use this book as a starting point for your personal growth journey, but always trust your judgment and seek professional advice when necessary.

By reading this document, the reader agrees that under no circumstances is the author or publisher responsible for any losses, direct or indirect, that are incurred as a result of the use of the information contained within this document, including, but not limited to, errors, omissions, or inaccuracies.

To Stephanie, Daniella, and Patrick,

My amazing children, you are the beating heart of this book. Your journeys from wide-eyed teens to confident, grounded adults have been my greatest inspiration and joy. Together, we've weathered the storms of growing up. Watching you emerge as the incredible individuals you are today fills your dad and me with immense pride.

This book is a testament to our shared experiences—the laughter, the tears, the triumphs, and the challenges we've faced together. It's a collection of wisdom born from your unique personalities, our family's resilience, and the love that has guided us through it all.

To the world, you're capable of extraordinary things. To me, you already are extraordinary. This book is for you, because of you, and inspired by you. May it serve as a reminder of our journey and the unwavering love that will always connect us.

With all my love and pride,

Mami

Table of Contents

Navigating the Journey to Adulthood — 9

Part One: North
Level Up

1. **UNCOVERING YOUR ESSENCE** — 15
   - Taking The Wheel — 16
   - The Four Pillars of Self-Discovery — 17
   - Overcoming Obstacles — 26
   - Charting Your Path Forward — 27

2. **DEVELOPING A GROWTH MINDSET** — 29
   - Level Up Your Mindset — 29
   - Resilience: The Answer to Failure and Setbacks — 34
   - What's Next? — 35

3. **CRAFTING YOUR FUTURE** — 37
   - Finding Your True North — 38
   - Choosing Your Path — 40
   - Decisions: Navigating Your Options — 46
   - Self-Discovery Toolkit — 48
   - Ready, Set, Go — 50

Part Two: East
Skill Up

4. **BECOMING UNSTOPPABLE** — 53
   - Why Does Learning Never Stop? — 54
   - How to Cultivate a Lifelong Learning Mindset — 54
   - Embracing Technology — 57
   - Staying Curious and Adaptable — 59
   - Balancing Technology Use — 60
   - The Takeaway — 63

5. **POWERING UP YOUR SOFT SKILLS** — 65
   - Priorities: Rock Your To-Do List — 66
   - Setting Boundaries: The Art of Saying No — 68
   - Time Management: Time Is Gold! — 70
   - Productivity: Moving the Needle — 71
   - Overcoming Productivity Zappers — 73
   - Communication: Much More than Saying It Right! — 76
   - Leadership: Walk Your Talk — 80

Skill Booster	82
Power Up Your Game	83

Part Three: South
Circle of Trust

6. BUILDING MEANINGFUL CONNECTIONS — 87
- The Hunger to Belong — 89
- Core Relationship Principles — 90
- The Role of Friends — 91
- Home Is Where the Heart Is — 94
- Role Models and Trusted Advisers — 97
- The Power of Networking — 98
- Building Your Inner Circle — 100
- Shielding Your Inner Circle — 102

7. MATTERS OF THE HEART — 103
- Love vs. Infatuation — 104
- Self-Love: The Foundation of Healthy Relationships — 105
- Red Flags — 106
- Nurturing Your Heart — 109

8. NAVIGATING RELATIONSHIP STORMS — 111
- Relationship Dynamics — 112
- Peer Pressure — 113
- Social Media Pressure — 114
- Conflict Resolution — 115
- Forgiveness and Moving Forward — 117
- EQ: Your Relationship Compass — 118
- Connection Corner — 121
- The Takeaway — 122

Part Four: West
Cash Course

9. MAKING BANK — 125
- What's Your Money Personality? — 126
- Banking Basics: Your Money's New Home — 127
- Credit: The Good, The Bad, and The Ugly — 129
- Interest Rates: A Two-Way Street — 132
- Saving, Not Borrowing — 132
- Income: Cash Coming In — 134
- Expenses: Money Going Out — 134
- Budgeting: Your Money's Game Plan — 135
- The Bottom Line: Money Management Is a Life Skill — 137

10. GROWING YOUR MONEY — 139
   Money Mindset: A Balanced Approach — 139
   Planting The Seeds of Wealth — 140
   Question What You Know — 144
   The Magic Formula — 146
   Investing vs. Speculating — 147
   Seeking Guidance and Taking Action — 148
   Money Matters — 150
   The Compass Points to Financial Independence — 152

Part Five: Center
Vibe Check

11. REACHING PEAK HEALTH — 155
    Youth Isn't Immunity — 155
    Trend to Dependency — 157
    Change Is Possible — 160
    Eat, Move, Thrive — 163
    Doing Something About It — 168

12. BUILDING YOUR MENTAL FORTRESS — 169
    Embracing Cognitive Behavioral Therapy (CBT) — 169
    Managing Mental Health Challenges — 172
    Other Ways to Take Care of Your Mind — 175
    Your Mental Health Matters — 177

13. NURTURING YOUR SOUL — 179
    The Power of Spiritual Health — 180
    Practical Steps for Spiritual Alignment — 182
    Wellness Corner — 184
    Balancing Mind, Body, and Soul — 186

   It's a Wrap! — 189
   References — 193

Navigating the Journey to Adulthood

Imagine standing at the helm of a small sailboat, the vast ocean of life stretching out like an endless blue canvas. The salty breeze of possibility whips through your hair as you adjust your sails and set your course. Your heart pounds with exhilaration and nervousness because once you leave the safe harbor of home, you'll be at the mercy of the untamed waters of adulthood.

Does this sound familiar? That's because embarking on the journey from teen years to adulthood is a lot like setting sail on a solo voyage. This modern-day odyssey will test your courage, resilience, and adaptability.

You might feel like you've been set adrift without a compass. Maybe you're stressed about school, confused about your future, or just going through the motions. The chaotic waves of social media, peer pressure, and societal expectations crash against your boat, threatening to capsize your sense of self.

On top of that, you're dealing with the quest for freedom, a deep hunger to belong, and the pursuit of fulfillment – all while navigating the complexities of our interconnected world. Trust me, I get it. Being a teenager or young adult these days is no joke.

You're trying to figure out who you are and what you want in a modern world that's changing faster than TikTok trends. It's like you're supposed to have it all figured out, but inside, you're thinking, "Um, can I get a manual for this whole life thing?"

Well, good news – you've just found your life compass.

You might wonder, "Who's this captain trying to guide my ship?" I'm not here to bark orders or pretend I have all the answers. Picture me as that seasoned sailor who's weathered a few storms and is eager to share the lessons learned. This book combines research-backed strategies, real-life examples, and practical advice I wish I had received at your age.

This book is not just a compass but also a map and a trusty cabin of supplies all rolled into one. It's not about giving you a step-by-step guide to becoming successful (sorry, no cheat codes here). Instead, it's about empowering you with the tools, mindset, and knowledge to craft your unique path to thriving.

Just like a compass has cardinal directions, our journey together will explore five key areas that'll help you navigate this wild adventure called life:

- **North: Level Up**—Get ready to discover your true self, uncover your passions, and tap into superpowers you didn't even know you had. We'll embrace a growth mindset that will have you crushing self-doubt like a bug.
- **East: Skill Up**—In a world that's changing faster than ever, we'll explore how to become a lifelong learner. You'll discover how to harness technology for good (not just endless scrolling) and sharpen those soft skills that'll set you apart in any situation.

- **South: Circle of Trust**—Let's talk about your crew: the heart of your support system. We'll dive into building a squad that lifts you higher (and how to stay away from toxic waters). You'll learn how to create and maintain deep, meaningful connections that can weather any storm.
- **West: Cash Course**—Adulting 101, anyone? Get the inside scoop on money matters like budgeting, investing, and viewing cash as a tool to craft the life of your dreams (not just for impulse buying). We're about to make finances fun – or at least less scary.
- **Center: Vibe Check**—A healthy you is at the core of it all. We'll explore balancing your physical, mental, and spiritual well-being.

🚀	Key skills or mindsets to master
💡	Interactive exercises to spark reflection
📓	Journal prompts for writing
⚠️	Cautions or "red flags" to watch for
🧠	Bonus resources

But fair warning: this isn't a passive read. We will dig deep, tackle tough questions, and challenge you to step outside your comfort zone. Get ready for thought-provoking journaling prompts, interactive activities, and real talk that might make you squirm. All good signs that indicate growth! Plus, you'll find QR codes throughout the book linking to additional resources, videos, and tools to supercharge your journey. Throughout the book, you'll find helpful icons serving as guideposts.

More than ever, the world needs your unique gifts, passion, and energy. But to change the world, you've got to start with yourself. This book is your toolkit for becoming the best version of you – someone who's confident, resilient, and ready to make waves (the good kind).

So, are you ready to set sail and embark on this epic voyage of self-discovery and growth? To navigate the unchartered waters of your potential and create a life that makes you want to jump out of bed in the morning (okay, after hitting snooze once or twice)?

Grab your favorite drink, find a comfy spot, and let's set sail. Your future self will be so thankful you picked up this compass.

It's time to find your true north and thrive. Let's do this!

Part One: North

LEVEL UP

The Fearless Explorer: *This character embodies the journal of self-awareness and personal growth. They are constantly exploring their passions, strengths, and values. With a growth mindset, they are resilient, confident, and know where to go. They embrace failure as a learning opportunity.*

ONE

Uncovering Your Essence

> *When you know yourself, you are empowered. When you accept yourself, you are invincible.*
>
> Tina Lifford

Have you ever felt like you're stuck on a merry-go-round, spinning endlessly without knowing why you hopped on in the first place? Or like a chameleon at a disco party, constantly shifting colors to blend in with the flashing lights? You may have bought the latest fashion trends or concert tickets for a band everyone raves about, more because of the fear of missing out than the desire to watch them perform.

Maybe it's peer pressure, FOMO, or just the chaos of life—but you may often find yourself conforming, even when it doesn't feel right. Whatever the reason, you may keep dancing to the beat of someone else's drum, wearing shoes that don't fit, and wondering why your feet hurt.

If this sounds familiar, you are not alone!

How Did You End Up Here?

But here's the deal: where you are now is just a pit stop on a journey filled with twists, turns, and uncovered destinations. Your past choices, environment, and experiences have shaped you, but they don't define your future. As you step into adulthood, it's time to grab the wheel and steer your own course.

Taking The Wheel

Before hitting the accelerator, let's calibrate our internal GPS. Discovering who you are is crucial to determining your direction in life. It's time to shift focus from "where you are" to "who you are." By developing self-awareness, you gain clarity about your origins and desired destinations.

Uncovering your passions, abilities, and life goals transforms you from a passive passenger to an active driver in your life's journey, steering the wheel toward "where you want to be."

Tell Me, Who Are You?

Let's get real. Have you ever really stopped, looked in the mirror, and asked, "Who am I?" Not with a glance or a quick check to see that there are no significant pimples or hairs out of place, but a deep dive into the core – quirks, emotions, beliefs, and hidden dreams? This exercise is not about vanity; it's about honesty. Soul-searching demands stripping away facades to confront the authentic self, imperfections, and all.

This honest self-assessment unlocks tremendous potential:

- Taking charge of one's life
- Building inner strength
- Creating authentic connections
- Pursuing passions with fire

Real talk: Self-knowledge paves the way to a desired life where you're in charge, eyes wide open to possibilities. On the flip side, ignoring the inner self can lead to falling into the same traps, wasting time, losing sight of what you want out of life, and missing the steps needed to get there.

Ready to unlock your potential? Grab pen and paper, and dig deep to uncover the real you. But hey, no pressure! This isn't about finding some perfect, final version of yourself. You're a work in progress – like we all are, and that's awesome to realize!

The key is to ask yourself the big questions and stay true to your path:

- What sparks a fire in your belly or snuffs it out?
- What gets you moving faster, or what makes you drag your feet?
- What gives you those "wow" chills or makes you uneasy?
- What can bring an instant smile to your face or a frown?
- What emotions do you wear on your sleeve, and what usually stirs them up?

Buckle up – your journey starts now!

The Four Pillars of Self-Discovery

Four components will empower you to clearly understand who you are. These are:

- **Your personality:** The essence of you.
- **Your values:** The "why" behind every decision and every move.
- **Your passions:** The "what" that sparks joy and energy in your life.
- **Your skills or talents:** The "how well" you do things, including those areas ripe for growth.

Let's take a deeper look at these pillars so you can see how they fit together and how you can harness them to make choices that enable you to lead a whole and authentic life.

Blueprint of Your Personality

Think of your personality as your very own signature—distinct and individual. It is the underlying code that programs how you think, feel, and act; just like your DNA gives you unique physical features, your personality gifts you with a blend of qualities that you were born with, for the most part. Some of these traits are also the effects of your environment and life experiences, but mainly your genetics.

The "Big Five": Most personality researchers agree that there are five primary personality traits (Goldberg 1990); think of these traits like a hand of cards dealt to you from the start. Each trait comprises a vast spectrum, and you may fall anywhere within this spectrum. An easy-to-remember acronym for the Big Five traits is OCEAN (Ackerman 2024). It stands for:

- **Openness to experience vs. closedness to experience:** People on the "open" side of the spectrum love trying out new experiences and crave novelty, while those nearer to the "closed" side prefer to stick to the familiar. Think about where you stand on this spectrum.
- **Conscientiousness vs. spontaneity:** Those on the more conscientious side of this spectrum are meticulous planners. They are organized and dependable and tend to finish things on time. Those on the spontaneous end wait until the last minute to do things and are more likely to go with the flow instead of meticulously planning their day or experiences. How about you?
- **Extraversion vs. introversion:** People known as extroverts feel energized in social situations, while those who are more introverted may feel drained by too much interaction and need more "me time." Do you look forward to occasions where you can meet new people or enjoy big parties where "everyone will be there"? Or does spending time at home reading or doing things with one or two close friends look more like your idea of a good time?
- **Agreeableness vs. competitiveness:** People on the most agreeable end of the spectrum are sometimes called "people pleasers." They prioritize getting along with others and find it easy to compromise. Those who are more competitive enjoy marching to the beat of their own drum and don't mind stepping on a few toes. Do you see yourself as more agreeable or competitive in your dealings with others?
- **Neuroticism vs. emotional stability:** People who are high in neuroticism can be prone to anxiety, low self-esteem, sadness, or worry. They can get angry quickly, temperamental, and feel self-conscious or unsure. Those on the low end of neuroticism/higher in emotional stability tend to feel confident, sure of themselves, and adventurous. They can show bravery and are not usually bogged down by self-doubt or worry. What about you? Are you

usually calm under pressure, cool as a cucumber, or do intense feelings sometimes get the best of you, making you feel stressed and often overwhelmed?

Within these spectrums, there is no "good" or "bad"—knowing where you stand simply means knowing yourself better and identifying the things that resonate with you. For instance, if you prefer smaller get-togethers and are shy about meeting new people, know it's okay to feel that way; or if you find that competitiveness is standing in the way of getting along with others while working on a group project, you can take vital steps to let others know you're on the same page.

When you know where you stand on the Big Five traits, you become more aware and less defensive in situations that are unnatural to your personality.

Your Core Values: What Things Matter the Most to You?

It's time to focus on the second pillar of self-discovery: your core values. Social media and our surroundings can sometimes impose irrelevant values on us. Looking and dressing a certain way, participating in "cool" activities, and even having a lot of money are often presented as the ultimate choices. But there is no ultimate "winner" when it comes to values.

Core values are the things that each person holds dear to themselves. They are principles that guide your everyday decisions and actions, and standing by them is vital if you want to be comfortable and authentic with yourself.

While personality is your nature, values are your choices (Fleming, 2023). Whether standing up for a friend, choosing to study over going out, or saying "no" when everyone else is saying "yes." These moments reflect your values.

> *When your values are clear, making decisions becomes easier.*
>
> Roy E. Disney

Let this quote simmer in your mind. Reflect on your day-to-day life: do you allow your values to shape your actions? And how might those actions be paving the way for your future? With these thoughts fresh in your mind, let's begin mapping out the values calling you.

Embark on Your Value Quest

Take your journal and write down what lights your fire. What would you stand up for, no matter what? What people/causes tug at your heartstrings? Use this starter list to brainstorm. But don't stop here—add anything and everything that rings true to you.

Authenticity	Family	Honesty	Love
Balance	Freedom	Humility	Peace
Creativity	Friendship	Inclusion	Relationships
Curiosity	Fun	Integrity	Wealth
Environment	Hard Work	Justice	Well-being
Faith	Helping Others	Leadership	Wisdom

Your "Nope" List

Now flip it—what are your absolute deal-breakers, the energy-zappers, the "not in a million years" things? List those, too. Dishonesty, unfairness, or simply the yawns of boredom?

Pinpointing these anti-values will help you set boundaries that help you live authentically and make the right decisions.

Admire and Aspire

Defining your core values takes time, and it's okay if they evolve. Look to those who inspire you – friends, family, mentors, celebrities, spiritual leaders, or fictional characters. What qualities do you admire in them?

These admired traits often reflect your own values. It could be your friend's compassion, your grandfather's unwavering principles, an athlete's determination, or an influencer's commitment to positivity. Recognize these qualities as silent cheerleaders guiding your own value system.

Add these inspiring attributes to your growing list of personal values. Remember, inspiration can come from anyone who touches your life meaningfully.

Reflect and Daydream

- **Peaks and valleys:** Reflect on your highest highs and lowest lows. What values anchored you or were missing?
- **Ideal day:** Visualize your perfect day from start to finish. What activities and interactions fill it? This reveals the things and people that matter the most to you.
- **Legacy:** Fast forward to the future. What impact do you want to have on the world? Let this guide your choices now.

Envisioning the legacy you wish to leave can be powerfully shaped by witnessing the profound effect one person's actions can have. I vividly remember attending my dad's funeral and being astonished by the outpouring of gratitude from all walks of life—from garbage collectors to high-powered executives, they were all there to pay their respects. One by one, they stepped forward to share stories of his generosity, his open-door policy, and his open heart.

You see, my dad was the kind of man who gave freely without expecting praise or accolades. His acts of kindness flew under the radar, as he was motivated by a genuine desire to uplift those around him. Whether lending a listening ear, providing financial assistance during tough times, or simply offering encouragement, he touched countless lives quietly yet impactfully.

His example taught me that true generosity isn't about grand gestures or public displays; it's about the simple, everyday acts of kindness that ripple outward, creating a lasting impact beyond our lifetime.

By vividly picturing the legacy you wish to create, you can align your daily choices with your long-term goals, ensuring that every step brings you closer to the life you want to achieve.

Seal the Deal with Your Core Values

The "Top Five": With a universe of values to choose from, there are a special few that you'll hold on to come rain or shine. These nonnegotiable values are the pillars of your creed. Picking your top five isn't about ticking the "right" boxes. It's about honoring those that click with your heart.

To help decide on your five core values, write your answer to the following questions (Therapist Aid, n.d.):

- What are the five values that society cherishes the most?
- What are the five values that my friends cherish the most?
- What are the five values that my family cherishes the most?
- What are the five values that I cherish the most?

Some values in each category overlap but don't necessarily have to. Reflect on your answers and think about how your values align with or differ from those of others. Go back to this list and add, delete, or tweak your values if any changes occur. You will discover a lot about yourself this way!

Passions: The Sparks That Drive You

Now, we come to the third pillar of what makes you unique: your passions. They are where your values come alive. Passions are the pursuits that make time disappear. Engaging in them makes you feel alive, happy, and fulfilled. Think about moments when you were "in the zone," doing something you loved. What were you doing? How did it make you feel? Keep exploring new things—your passions may evolve over time. Stay open and curious.

Often, our passions are extensions of our values. For instance, if one of your top values is helping others, your passions might lead you toward volunteer work, teaching, or medicine.

Let's explore what activities energize and light you up and how these connect to your values.

Here is a starter pack to help spark your imagination. Feel free to expand.

Arts & Crafts	Entrepreneurship	Nature	Teaching
Cars	Fashion	Numbers	Technology
Dance	Health and Fitness	Photography	Travel
Debating	History	Psychology	Video Production
Design	Law	Reading	Volunteering
Education		Sports	Writing

Evaluate and Reflect

As you participate in various activities, pause to analyze your emotional responses. Create a simple chart or journal entry after each new experience. Ask yourself: Did this activity energize or drain me? Did I lose track of time, or was I watching the clock? Did it feel like a chore, or could I do this all day? Journaling these feelings will help you discern which activities genuinely resonate with your passions and which might not fit.

Discovering Your Superpowers

We've arrived at the fourth pillar that will help unlock your essential self. This pillar is centered on discovering your unique talents—let's call them your superpowers! Think about the skills or abilities that feel as easy as scrolling through your feed. They come as naturally as breathing and make you stand out in the crowd. When you do something that clicks, it's empowering, right? That's your superpower in action.

Take, for example, the art of writing. How do the words flow for you? Can you craft a story that pulls readers in? Or say you do sports; do you find that your reflexes are super quick and that you can dribble a basketball or catch a football in flight so fast that you help your team achieve a winning score? What about making friends? Do you find it easy to meet new people, and have people often told you you're a good listener?

Reflecting on questions like these will help identify your strengths. But let's be honest—everyone has their kryptonite, too. Maybe staying focused in class trips you up… or do you find it hard to express your anger calmly and assertively? Acknowledging your strengths and weaknesses allows you to identify areas you can work on to transform "not yet" into "nailed it."

Spotlighting Your Superpowers

Which ones resonate with you?

Artist	Empathetic	Musician	Responsible
Athlete	Great Listener	Organizer	Singer
Communicator	Innovator	Patient	Sociable
Cool-headed	Leader	Planner	Storyteller
Dependable	Loyal	Punctual	Team Player
Driven	Math Wizz	Quick Study	Writer

Have I missed anything that you can identify with?

Celebrating Your Strengths

Now that you've identified your strengths, you can take a moment to appreciate them. Yes, you can take a victory lap. Even if you're still developing some areas, remember that every skill you possess is a win worth celebrating. Every day provides an opportunity to create new strengths and work on the parts you feel might be holding you back, whether in academics, sports, or relationships.

Expanding Your Horizons

Consider this the start of your personal treasure hunt. Whether you're a strategy guru or a blossoming artist, there's always new terrain to explore and new skills to refine. Use your existing talents as a launchpad to reach higher levels of mastery.

Remember, the path to excellence is always under construction—there's always a higher peak to strive for. Keep challenging yourself to improve and shine brighter in all you do—don't settle!

The Other Side of Your Superpowers

Now that you've looked in the mirror and seen who's staring back at you, it's time to take the microscope and look a bit closer!

It's often easier to focus on the good parts and ignore the pimples and warts. Sure, you could just hit "skip" on the tricky parts, but where's the growth? Imagine a bodybuilder who only works on their upper body. Sure, they'll have great biceps and well-defined abs, but they'll only have matchsticks to stand on, and they're only half as strong as they could be.

The same goes for you. Focusing on your weak spots isn't a downer—it's an opportunity to identify growth areas. Now, let's consider that "work-in-progress" starter list:

Anxious	Fear of Rejection	Insecure	Overthink Things
Chatty in Class	Gloomy	Immature	Possessive
Clutter Bug	Headstrong	Jealous	Procrastinator
Ball of Emotions	Impatient	Lack of Focus	Struggle Communicating
Fear of Failure	Impulsive	Lack of Motivation	

Valuing Your Imperfections

> There is a crack in everything; that's how the light gets in.
>
> Leonard Cohen

In a world that often seeks perfection, there's unique value in embracing your imperfections. These aren't flaws to discard but opportunities for incredible growth.

I love this story because it illustrates this idea brilliantly:

Once, a man had to carry two buckets to fetch water from a distant well. One bucket had a crack, causing it to be empty by the time he reached home. The cracked bucket felt sad for not being helpful. The man explained that he knew about the crack all along. He planted seeds along the path. "Didn't you notice beautiful flowers on your side of the track?" The crack allowed water to seep out, watering the seeds and growing beautiful flowers that brightened his day.

This story shows that our imperfections can lead to unexpected and positive outcomes. It teaches us that our weaknesses can sometimes create opportunities and bring beauty to the world in ways we might not initially recognize. Embracing our imperfections allows us to see the hidden potential and value they bring to our lives and the lives of others. Often, they help us understand others better when they aren't being their best selves.

Remember, strengths and weaknesses aren't set in stone. You can always learn and grow. Embrace your superpowers and see "weaknesses" as opportunities to level up.

Congrats—you've explored the four pillars of self-discovery: personality, values, passions, and skills. They all interconnect to paint a picture of who you are.

Overcoming Obstacles

Self-discovery is a rewarding yet challenging journey. Expect a few curveballs along the way. Here are some common obstacles and tips for navigating them:

- **Self-doubt and negative self-talk:** Celebrate small victories and progress and pay attention to the moments when you're telling yourself negative things like "I'm just not good at school" or "Nobody likes me." Reframe your negative thoughts into useful ones like, "I didn't do well on this test, but that's okay. Next time, I'll start studying one week before the exam. I did well using a study timetable last time, and I can do so again." You might also say, "I haven't made any friends at my new school yet. Tomorrow, I'll ask Jen if I can have lunch with her. She seemed nice and welcoming and smiled warmly when I walked into class."

- **Conflicting opinions:** Respect different viewpoints but stay true to your values and beliefs. Don't take things personally when others disagree with you.
- **Changing interests or passions:** Embrace shifts as natural parts of personal growth. Let go of what no longer serves you, and be open to exploring new avenues.
- **Struggling with specific aspects of self-discovery:** Seek support from trusted individuals to provide honest feedback on your true self.
- **The pressure to fit in:** Recognize the immense pressure to fit and societal expectations, but prioritize authenticity.
- **Be aware of your starting point:** Have you ever heard the saying, "You were born in third base, but you believe you hit a triple?" When you're "born on third base," you already have a considerable advantage. All you need to do is run to home plate to score. If you feel ahead of your peers, aim to acknowledge that your starting position is influenced by factors like upbringing and socioeconomic status. Use this awareness to remain humble and help others advance.

Understand that your journey toward self-discovery is rarely linear. Embrace twists and turns, stay committed, view challenges as learning opportunities, and trust the process of personal growth and becoming your best self.

Charting Your Path Forward

With all the new knowledge you have obtained about yourself, I hope you are stepping off the carousel of passive existence and actively grabbing the reins of your life. That compass needle might swing a little to the left or the right over the next few months and years, but at least you know you're headed in the right general direction for now.

Discovering who you are is vital to knowing which direction to steer in: your True North. By being self-aware, you gain clarity and insight into where you come from and where you want to go. Now, you are ready to equip yourself with a power hack to help you grow, expand, and stay on track. Want to know more? Keep reading to find out.

TWO

Developing a Growth Mindset

> *I've missed more than 9000 shots in my career. I've lost almost 300 games. Twenty-six times, I've been trusted to take the game-winning shot and missed. I've failed over and over and over again in my life. And that is why I succeed.*
>
> Michael Jordan

At fifteen, Michael Jordan didn't make his high school varsity team. The coach didn't see his potential, and he grew devastated, almost quitting. But, with relentless practice and his mother's encouragement, he became one of the greatest basketball players ever. Today, Michael Jordan is an NBA legend with six championships and countless accolades, but his journey was far from smooth.

His secret? Seeing setbacks as opportunities to learn and grow. He had a growth mindset!

Level Up Your Mindset

Have you ever caught yourself saying, "I can't do this," or "I'm just not good at that?" Or the classic, "I wasn't born with that gene?" These are signs of a fixed mindset, a perspective that can limit your potential and success.

Our surroundings have enforced this fixed mindset since early on. In school, if you scored low grades, you were a failure, or if you did not make the star team, you were not good enough. Furthermore, people may be labeled as "good at writing, but not at math" or similar.

Psychologist Carol Dweck, who developed the concept of "growth mindset," found that many beliefs we tell ourselves (or hear from others) about our abilities are simply untrue (Dweck, 2006). She observed that some students quickly gave up when faced with challenges, while others showed remarkable resilience and enthusiasm for difficult tasks.

Dweck's research revealed that a key element of success in life is having a "growth mindset" – the belief that abilities, skills, and intelligence can be developed through effort, learning, and persistence.

Let's look at a helpful summary of how people with fixed vs. growth mindsets view the world.

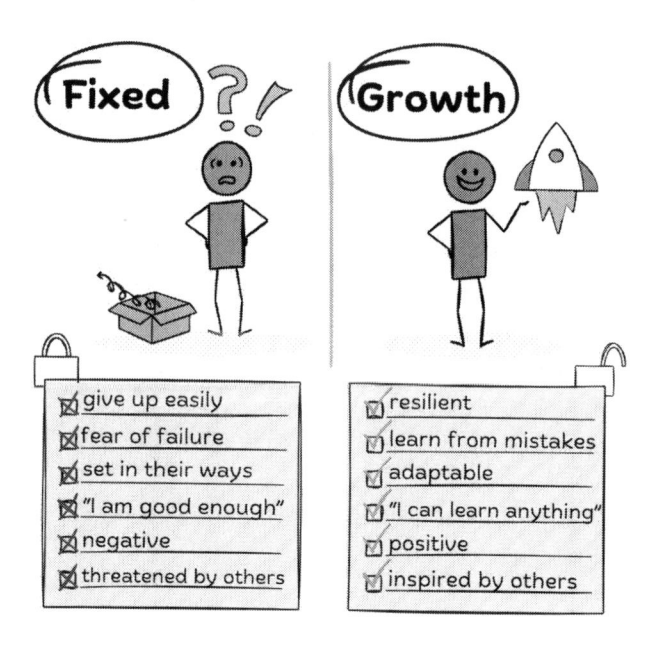

Fixed	Growth
give up easily	resilient
fear of failure	learn from mistakes
set in their ways	adaptable
"I am good enough"	"I can learn anything"
negative	positive
threatened by others	inspired by others

People with fixed mindsets:

- Believe their abilities are set in stone; they are either naturally talented or not.
- Think if you need to try hard, you're not intelligent enough.

- If they are great at sports, feel superior, and do not think they must try harder.
- Can't stop showing off their achievements to feel superior.
- Act stubbornly and resist change, sticking to what they know.
- See challenges as threats.
- Feel threatened by others' success, thinking it highlights their failures.
- Individual (not team) performance comes first.
- Believe that making an effort is pointless.
- Setbacks are failures.
- They are critical of themselves and their circumstances.
- Complain and blame others for their situation.
- When teased or bullied, they feel victimized and resentful and seek revenge.
- See success as measured by wealth, power, or fame.

On the flip side, people with growth mindsets:

- Are resilient—they bounce back quickly from mistakes, "failures," or disappointments.
- They believe they can get more intelligent and better at anything with hard work and persistence.
- They feel talent is just the starting point.
- They are humble about success. Credit the team even when they've done most of the work.
- See setbacks as lessons.
- View challenges as opportunities.
- Are adaptable—able to find new ways to tackle issues and change direction.
- See skills as buildable.
- Believe that effort is the path to mastery.
- They are optimistic—they see problems as opportunities to learn and grow.
- Are inspired by others' success—using it as motivation rather than feeling threatened.
- They are most excited when the team does well.
- When teased or bullied, tries to understand the other's perspective and helps them change.
- Define success by their own ideals, not others'.

Adopting a growth mindset frees you from this fixed pattern of thinking. It enables you to embrace the idea that anything you haven't mastered comes with a big "yet." There is always time to learn, grow, and perfect… and doing so is one of the key elements of success in all realms of your life —your school, future career, and relationships.

Studies have shown that individuals with a growth mindset tend to:

- Perform better academically
- Experience less depression and anxiety
- Exhibit fewer behavioral problems (Yeager et al., 2019)

This research underscores the significant impact that our mindset can have on various aspects of our lives, from academic achievement to mental health.

How to Develop a Growth Mindset

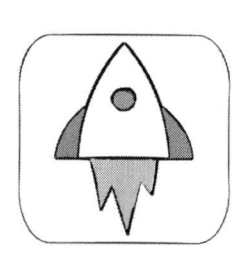

How do you stop your brain from switching off when there's a failure? How do you train your mind to light up at the prospect of challenges? The good news is, according to scientific research (Villas-Boas, 2022), brains are malleable. They can reshape and grow new connections, which means you can retrain your brain!

Let's discover handy strategies that will help you develop a growth mindset:

- **Recognize traps.** Recognize fixed mindset thoughts and reframe them. Notice negative self-talk like "I'm terrible at math!" Catch and flip it: "Math is challenging, but I'm still learning."
- **Accept challenges.** Embrace challenges as opportunities to stretch and grow. One good way to embrace challenges is to list the things you fear from one to five (from least to most feared). Select an item at around level one or two. Commit to choosing one item from your list every week or every month, and try to go up one level and another as the days, weeks, or months go by!
- **Don't fear failure.** Learn from them. Ask, "What can I improve?" rather than saying, "I'm a failure." Thomas Edison once said, "I didn't fail 1000 times. The lightbulb was an invention with 1000 steps."

- **Reward effort.** See effort as the key to mastery. Celebrate the process, not just the results. If you studied hard for a test, congratulate yourself by doing something you love, even before grades are posted!
- **Continue learning.** Beware the "everybody gets a trophy" syndrome. Just trying isn't enough if you're not learning and advancing. Evaluate, adjust, and advance.
- **Cultivate resilience and flexibility.** Think of a Weeble toy: no matter how hard you punch it, it always stands upright because of its design to keep its balance!
- **Encourage persistence.** Giving up is a hallmark of a fixed mindset. You need to push through barriers and reach the other side to grow.
- **Know when to quit.** Identify the difference between:

  o *A Lack of Effort:* When you give up because you didn't put in enough effort, quitting is the easy way out. This may feel good in the short term, but it can make you lose confidence in yourself in the long run.

  o *Changing Direction:* This is when you quit because you realize the direction you were heading in wasn't leading to your desired outcome, and continuing would be a waste of time. It is a well-thought decision that does not come from a place of fear but of calm reasoning.

- **Surround yourself with positive people.** Many criticize others and the world without offering solutions. You know who they are! Seek advice, feedback, and inspiration from growth-minded people and inspiration. Don't let negativity rub off on you.
- **Stay positive.** Being positive isn't about faking a smile; it's about being brave and believing in the benefits of facing difficulties head-on, knowing you can grow from them.
- **Embrace vulnerability and share your emotions.** Feeling scared, vulnerable, or out of your depth is okay because that makes you real. When you are honest about what you think and feel, it's easier to recognize that you must do something to overcome these feelings and emotions.

Resilience: The Answer to Failure and Setbacks

Here's some shocking news: You're going to fail! It might sound hostile and harsh, but it's the truth. And it's okay to do so! Everyone faces storms of different kinds that challenge and test them. Ignoring these challenges and sticking your head in the sand like an ostrich doesn't help. Similarly, fighting every obstacle head-on might make you feel strong. Still, it can also make you stubborn and unable to grow.

We can agree that failure is inevitable but not the end. Becoming resilient is the name of the game. But how? Here are a few tips (White-Gibson, 2022):

- **Pause:** Your feelings and emotions can get the better of you after suffering defeat. Anger, disappointment, and guilt are all bubbling up, about to explode. Pause and breathe before reacting. Recognize the pain of these emotions and use them as motivation for change.
- **Accept:** Right now, you can't do anything to change the outcome. If you lost a soccer game yesterday, it's over for now. If you failed a test today, you can't change the result. The key is identifying what you can control vs. what is out of your control. Accept the current reality and focus on what you can control going forward.
- **Reframe:** Instead of beating yourself up over everything that went wrong, step back in your mind and see it as a puzzle that needs to be solved. What happened in the past doesn't necessarily dictate what will happen in the future! Shift from a negative mindset to a positive one.
- **Plan:** Look at your past mistakes. What could you have done better? Identify weak points and decide what needs to happen to overcome those areas. Make a list and identify solutions for each one. Then, put your plan into action! Make a plan to apply those lessons forward. Small steps build momentum.
- **Connect:** Getting back up is hard when you must do it alone. Sometimes, when you fall, the only way to stand up again is to grab someone else's hand so they can help you get onto your feet. Connect with supportive people who encourage your growth.
- **Get skilled:** Pick up the skills to get things done differently. For instance, if you have a lot to memorize for a test, create a study plan, use mind maps and online tools, commit to listing down items you are having difficulty with, and ask for help if needed. In this example, simply by adopting better study habits (new skills),

you can make a big difference in your grades. If things are not working as they are, the last thing you want to do is keep repeating the same and expect different results. Try different strategies so you never feel stuck!

What's Next?

Embracing a growth mindset is transformative. It means seeing challenges as adventures, effort as the path to mastery, and failure as a launchpad for learning. With this lens, nothing can hold you back. You're ready to tackle any obstacle and evolve into your best self.

Now, you know who you are. You are ready to push through and grow. But which way? Which path will suit you the best? Step forward with courage and determination. The adventure awaits!

THREE

Crafting Your Future

> *My interest is in the future because I will spend the rest of my life there.*
>
> Charles Kettering

As you approach your late teens, you may reflect on the last couple of years and think, "Wow! They just flew by!" One second, you're aching because your BFF didn't invite you to their sleepover, and the next, you're freaking out about college applications.

Breathe easy. You don't need to have it all figured out right now. The secret sauce is to keep exploring, staying true to yourself, seeking support, and making informed decisions.

Looking back at my teen years, it's almost comical how many times I changed my mind about my future. One minute, I was dead set on becoming a doctor; the next, I sketched building designs and dreamed of becoming an architect. Fast forward to today, and I'm neither!

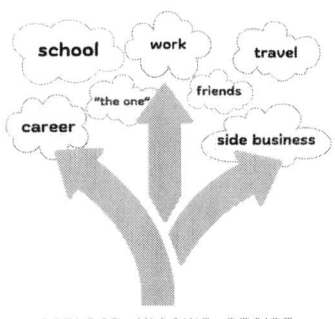

REFLECT, IMAGINE, DECIDE.

This constant flip-flopping isn't just a "me" thing. Most of my old classmates live lives totally different from what we imagined in high school. And you know what? That's the beauty of growing up and learning. Your interests will evolve. Recognizing when it's time to change direction is a superpower in itself. Staying open to these changes and opportunities is critical until you stumble across the one thing that lights you up so much you might end up dedicating your whole life to it!

From picking your classes to choosing a college, saying yes (or no!) to relationships, and even making those first big purchases – we've got you covered. This chapter will help you navigate these choices to craft your future confidently and clearly. Let's dive in!

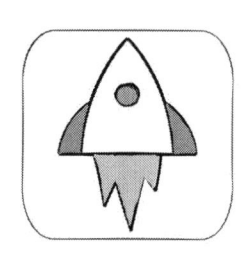

Finding Your True North

Your True North is your life's calling—the sweet spot where your talents, passions, and desire to make a difference align. It's like a compass guiding you towards a fulfilling life. While some folks wander through life without finding their calling, you're already ahead of the game by thinking about it.

Imagine waking up every day pumped about what you're going to do—that's what discovering your calling feels like! Are you ready to find your True North?

The Three Factors of Your Calling

Take your journal and make a list of each of these factors:

Strengths

These are your natural talents and abilities – things you excel at effortlessly. They're often what people compliment you on or tasks you do well without much struggle. Think back to the personality and skills exercises from Chapter One.

For example, you're great at organizing events, solving math problems, or understanding biology.

Passions

These are activities or subjects that deeply interest and fulfill you. Drawn from your values and passions explored in Chapter One, they make you lose track of time, fill you with excitement, and leave you wanting more. Passion is your fuel. What do you love doing so much that you'd do it all day, even for free?

It could be caring for animals, helping others, or playing sports.

Influence

This is how you want to positively impact others. Where can your actions or words change lives, communities, or industries? What problems do you want to solve? Which communities or groups would you like to serve or support?

Perhaps you want to raise awareness for animal shelters or improve animal well-being.

The Sweet Spot: Your Calling

Here is a fun exercise to visualize your calling:

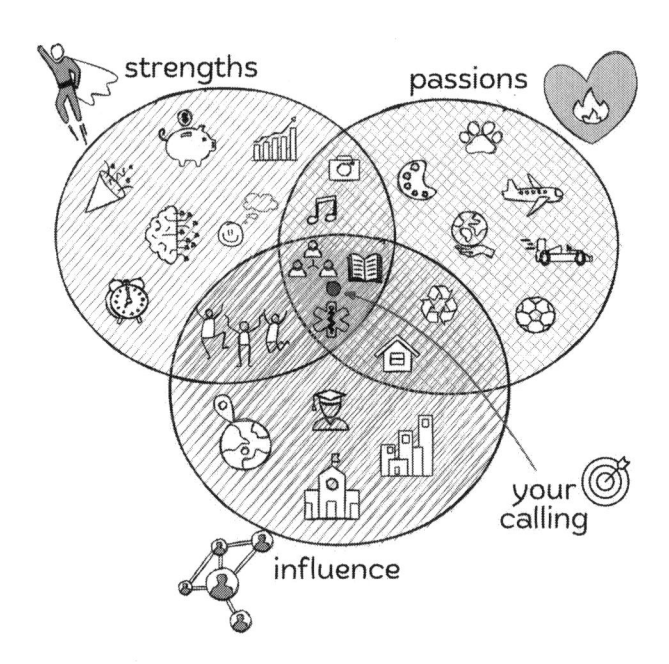

1. Draw three large overlapping circles.
2. Label each circle: Strengths, Passions, and Influence.
3. Place a dot on your diagram based on your strengths, passions, and interests in the corresponding circle. The closer a dot is to the center (where all circles overlap), the more it aligns with all three factors.

The sweet spot? That's right in the middle where all three circles meet. That's your potential calling!

For example, if your strength is organizing events, your passion is helping animals, and you want to impact animal well-being, your calling might be organizing fundraising events for animal shelters.

Making It Work

It's crucial to consider whether your calling can support you financially. If not, look for alternatives that combine your factors in a viable career.

For instance, if your strength is biology, your passion is helping animals, and you want to improve animal health, becoming a veterinarian could be financially feasible. As a vet, you could still organize events to support animal shelters to complement your practice.

Do some digging into career options that align with your sweet spot. Start exploring through side gigs, volunteering, shadowing, or internships. This hands-on experience will help you determine if your sweet spot is truly sweet and guide you in developing the necessary skills and expertise for success.

Finding your True North is an adventure, not a quick sprint. Don't sweat it if things aren't crystal clear right away or your compass needle wobbles as you grow and learn. The key is to stay curious, open to opportunities, and true to yourself as you navigate your path.

Choosing Your Path

You can make better decisions when you know "who you are" and "what you want." Sometimes, you might have to take risks, especially if your heart pulls you in a different direction from the crowd. Trust your compass – it will point to the route meant for you.

Once you've identified your calling, it's time to explore the paths to get there:

Career

Align your calling with your profession.

Our neighbor, David, got into coding as a kid and started freelancing as a web developer. His hands-on experience, analytical skills, and entrepreneurial spirit convinced him to study computer science and begin down this path. He eventually got hired by Microsoft, and he is killing it! Whether you see yourself as a scientist, artist, entrepreneur, or something else, the professional world is brimming with opportunities to match your calling with your career.

- **Explore your options:** Broaden your horizons.

    o Research job sites for in-demand skills.
    o Watch industry videos and talk to professionals.
    o Think beyond traditional career paths.

- **Consider your lifestyle fit:** Careers differ significantly in work hours, travel requirements, stress levels, and work-life balance. Find a career that matches your desired lifestyle.

    o For example, if you value flexibility, look into remote or hybrid work options or freelance careers.

- **Look to the future:** Consider long-term viability and growth potential.

    o Research industry trends and employment projections.
    o Consult school career advisers for insights on emerging fields.

- **Be open and flexible:** Your initial career choice isn't set in stone.

    o Embrace self-discovery and changing interests.
    o Consider taking general courses if undecided in college.
    o Be mindful of costs when switching paths.
    o Seek support and make research-based decisions to keep your expenditure to a minimum.

School

Choose an educational path that helps you achieve your dream job. Think about the academic institution where you see yourself thriving: college, trade school, online courses, or something else?

Here are a few tips to consider when exploring educational options:

- Identify your goals and interests.
- Is it financially feasible? Investigate cost, financial aid, and scholarships.
- Consider academic programs and offerings.
- Explore campus culture and community. Seek student feedback instead of relying solely on what schools promote online.
- Assess location and living situation. Roommates or solo? Town or city? Consider food and transportation costs.
- Evaluate: local, out-of-state, or abroad?
- Seek guidance and mentorship.
- Consider future prospects, such as your average salary once you graduate.

Fun fact: The US's average federal student loan debt is around $37,850. The average bachelor's degree graduate would take around ten years to pay off their student loan if they made debt repayments of $300 a month (Welding 2024). The upside to this is the fact that education does pay off. For instance, the median annual income of someone with less than a high school diploma is around $60,800. Compare that to someone with a master's degree, earning a median yearly salary of $90,300. The difference is quite significant (US Bureau of Labor Statistics n.d.).

Work Experience

Working as a teen is much more than just making money for your social lifestyle. Gaining practical experience, even if it seems unrelated to your career goals, provides invaluable opportunities to develop essential skills and connections. When you secure a job, even in a field that does not interest you, treat it as a chance to learn, grow, and make meaningful contributions.

Keep in mind that you're still developing your skills and knowledge, so your contributions to the company might be limited. However, this doesn't mean you can't add value. Focus on developing these key attributes that employers value in all industries, regardless of your experience level:

- **Curious and resourceful:** Be open to new experiences and show initiative by being resourceful.
- **Respectful:** Always maintain a respectful attitude towards colleagues and customers.
- **Reliable:** Showing up consistently and on time demonstrates your commitment and work ethic.

These initial jobs, whether selling coffee or interning at a local business, are stepping stones that help you build a professional network. They offer a platform to showcase your abilities, learn about workplace dynamics, and gain confidence in your capabilities. At the very least, the aim is to collect a good recommendation letter. By impressing your supervisors and staying in touch with colleagues, you're laying the groundwork for future opportunities. Remember, no matter how small, every job contributes to your personal and professional growth, preparing you for more advanced roles in your desired field.

Let's dive into a few ideas for building up your work experience:

- **Internships:** Internships can significantly affect your future. According to the State of Millennial Hiring Report (Vinay 2020), around 81% of graduates believe internships improve career prospects and often result in higher starting salaries.
- **Part-time jobs:** Securing a part-time job in a field you're passionate about can help build relevant skills and provide practical insights into the profession. It can also help you save and pay for your education.
- **Job shadowing:** Ask professionals in your desired field if you can shadow them. This lets you observe the work environment, daily tasks, and challenges firsthand.
- **Volunteering:** An excellent way to gain experience, especially in healthcare, social services, or education. It allows you to connect and learn from others while paying it forward.
- **Extracurricular activities:** Participation in school clubs, sports teams, or organizations that match your interests can offer significant practical experience and leadership opportunities. For

example, aspiring writers, journalists, and graphic designers can hone their skills by joining the school newspaper and using the articles they write or design to build a portfolio.

These activities and experiences are also excellent for beefing up your resumé, as they show that you are a go-getter keen on your area of interest.

Traveling

Ready to pack your bags for the adventure of a lifetime? Traveling isn't just about collecting Instagram-worthy snapshots. It's a thrilling experience of self-discovery that can supercharge your personal growth and even boost your grades! Yep, you heard that right – the Student & Youth Travel Association found that exploring the world can actually improve your academic performance (Springer, 2019).

Learning about new cultures, environments, and languages is a highly sought-after skill in today's interconnected world. It can stretch your horizons, challenge your perspectives, and ignite newfound passions.

Our family friend, Sophie, took a gap year after high school to volunteer at an orphanage and study Spanish in South America. This experience broadened her worldview and sparked an interest in international development, shaping her future academic path.

Before embarking on a trip, consider the following:

- **Reflect on your goals.** Are you seeking cultural immersion, personal growth, or adventure?
- **Research your destination.** Understand the local customs, language, weather, living accommodations, and travel requirements.
- **Safety.** Dig deep into local safety concerns, avoid risky areas, and stay vigilant. Keep emergency contacts handy, and always let key people know your location.
- **Emergency plan.** Purchase travel insurance, memorize important phone numbers, and carry extra cash. Know your embassy's location and local emergency services.
- **Plan.** Create an itinerary, balancing structured activities with free time for exploration. Figure out your financial needs and start saving early.

- **Set a budget.** Factor in transportation, accommodation, food, and activities – and don't forget currency exchange!
- **Working and studying.** Explore study abroad programs or international internships. Check requirements for work/study opportunities and consider exchange programs.
- **Embrace the local culture.** Step out of your comfort zone, try new food, attend local festivals, and connect with locals. Travel is an excellent opportunity to establish lifelong friendships.
- **Seek support.** While solo traveling can be rewarding, it's crucial to have a support system in place. Consider group tours or travel programs. Connect with other travelers or locals online.

Documenting your experiences through a journal, photographs, or blog can help you preserve memories, stay connected, and facilitate personal growth.

Business

Ever dreamed of turning your passion into profit? You can start today, just like my niece Emily did. She noticed local businesses struggling with social media and launched her digital marketing venture. Not only did she help these businesses thrive online, but she also picked up essential skills like client communication and project management. The best part? She funded most of her college degree, avoiding the dreaded student debt trap!

Emily's story isn't just inspiring – it's a blueprint for your entrepreneurial journey. Whether you're a coding whiz, a wordsmith, a tutor in the making, or have a knack for event planning, there's a business idea waiting to be born. The digital age has thrown open the doors to endless opportunities, often with little to no startup costs.

Successful businesses **solve problems**. So, put on your thinking hat and keep your eyes wide open. What needs aren't being met in your community or areas of interest? That gap could be your golden ticket.

Before you dive in, though, let's talk strategy:

- **Develop a business plan**, including:

    - What product or service are you offering?
    - Who is your target audience?
    - Who is your competition?

- What sets you apart from the competition?
- How are you going to market your offering?
- Projections of costs, expenses, revenue (sales), and expected profit (how much are you planning to make).
- How much time, effort, and money are needed?
- Check out the QR code at the end of the chapter for teen-friendly tools.

- **Start small** and test the waters.
- **Build your support network.**
- **Manage your finances wisely** (we'll dive deeper into this later).
- **Never stop learning.**
- **Hustle hard!** Spoiler alert: nothing comes easy; you must put in the time and effort to succeed.
- **Protect your intellectual property** (that's where patents, copyrights, and trademarks come in).

Remember that having a side income will be extremely valuable in complementing your costs of education, traveling, or other passions and interests in the future. To boost your confidence in your chosen pursuit, tap into your network for support – family, career counselors, mentors, and professionals in your field of interest. They can provide valuable insights, advice, and connections to help you navigate this exciting new world.

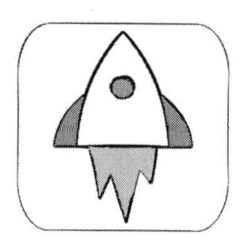

Decisions: Navigating Your Options

Not all choices are created equal. Some are as simple as picking between Netflix or TikTok for your evening entertainment. Others? They're the heavyweight champions of decisions—like choosing your college major, deciding whether to take that gap year to backpack across Europe. Or the big one: picking your life partner.

Every choice involves trade-offs. Every "yes" often comes with a silent "no" to something else. But don't let that paralyze you! The secret is aligning your choices with your values and embracing what makes you uniquely "you."

Decision Time

To become a master decision-maker, follow these key steps:

1. **Define the problem:** What's really at stake here?
Example: "Should I apply for the summer internship or attend a music camp?"
2. **Brainstorm solutions:** Get creative and explore all angles.
Example: Research both options, talk to past participants, and consider a split schedule.
3. **Weigh your options**: List the potential pros and cons.
For example, an Internship offers career experience, but a music camp aligns with your passion.
4. **Consider the consequences:** Think short-term and long-term.
Example: An internship might boost your resume, but a music camp would be fun and could lead to lifelong connections in the industry.

> **Pro tips:**
> o *Mental time travel:* This strategy involves traveling to the future and past. Imagine "Future You" looking back on this decision. What would you say? Involve "Past You" to weigh in on learned experiences to guide your choices.
> o *Scenario planning:* Consider all possible outcomes, including each option's best and worst-case scenarios. (Duke, 2018)

5. **Trust your gut:** While facts and data are essential, don't ignore your instincts. If a decision feels wrong, pay attention to that intuition.

6. **Seek advice:** Get feedback from trusted sources who have your best interests in mind and can offer different perspectives, but remember— you own the decision and its consequences.

There is no such thing as a crystal ball for decision-making. You won't always nail the "perfect" choice, and it's totally okay! The game-changer is having a solid system in your toolbox to help you make intelligent, well-thought-out decisions. It's about swapping those impulsive, "feels right in the moment" choices for ones you've invested some brain power into.

And here's the bonus: when you make informed decisions, you're not just hoping for the best – you're preparing for everything. You won't be blindsided if things don't go exactly as planned (they often don't). Remember those worst-case scenarios you thought through? They've already prepared you emotionally for bumps in the road. So, instead of feeling knocked off your feet, you'll be ready to roll with the punches and adapt confidently, knowing you've already considered and prepared for them.

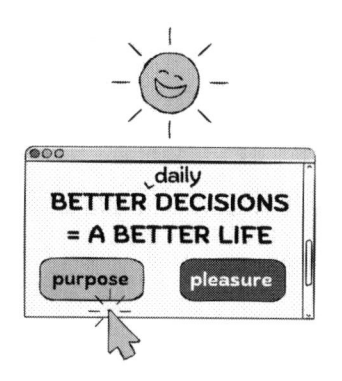

Next time you're faced with a big decision, take a deep breath, pull out your toolbox, and trust in your ability to make the best call with what you've got.

Self-Discovery Toolkit

Self-discovery is an ongoing journey. Use these tools regularly to refine your understanding and stay true to your evolving self.

Reflection and Journaling

- How do your passions align with your values?
- How do your skills support your passions?
- What were the high and low energy points of my day?
- Did I encounter any challenges? How did I respond?
- How did I step out of my comfort zone, and what did I learn?
- What values were reflected in my decisions today? How did I feel?
- Did I lose track of time doing something today? Or did it feel like chores?
- What activities came naturally to me? And which ones made me tense up?
- Did someone inspire me today? Why?
- What diverse experience can I pursue to uncover hidden passions?
- What do others say about my strengths and weaknesses?
- Make a list of your top 5 strengths.
- Make a list of your top 5 passions.
- List ways you want to impact others. Which groups would you like to support?
- Reflect on a time you made a difficult decision. What factors did

you consider? How did it turn out? What did you learn from the experience?
- My biggest failure taught me...
- When I face a challenge, I will tell myself...
- To be more resilient, I will start...
- A role model who embodies a growth mindset is... because...

Future Visioning

- Imagine your ideal future 10 years from now. Describe your career, lifestyle, and accomplishments. What steps can you take today to work towards that vision?
- Create a vision board with images and quotes representing your goals and values. Use it as a daily reminder and motivation tool.

Unlock Your Bonus Self-Discovery Toolkit

Scan the QR code below to access additional resources, including worksheets, videos, recommended tools and apps, online self-assessment tests, and bonus tips and strategies. Check back often for updates and fresh content. Let's keep leveling up together!

Ready, Set, Go

You've taken the first steps on an exciting journey of self-discovery and future planning. Stay calm: finding your True North isn't a race – it's a lifelong adventure. If you're still in the process of figuring things out, that is perfectly okay. In fact, it's more than okay – it's normal and expected!

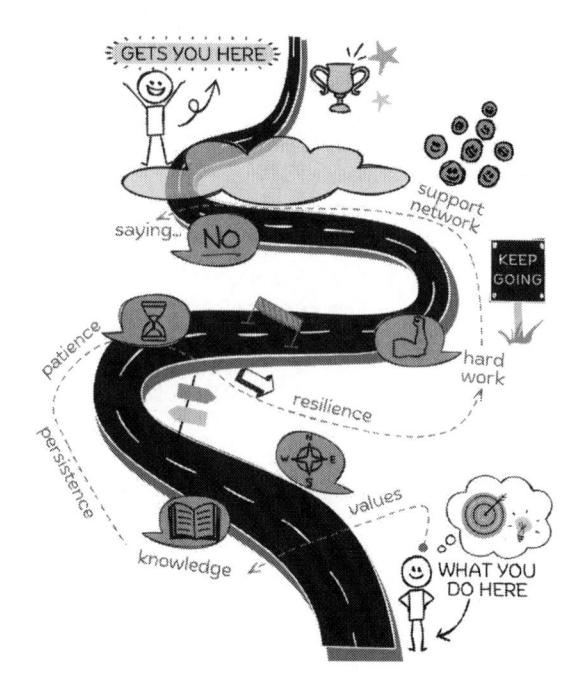

Remember, life is a winding road. Embrace it with patience, persistence, resilience, listening to your true self, and cheering squad. You will get there!

Your future is a canvas; you're the artist, equipped with the tools and insights to create your masterpiece. Stay curious, dream big, and enjoy the ride. The best is yet to come!

Next, we dive into 'skilling up,' where you'll sharpen your tools to add vibrant colors and intricate details to your life's journey. Turn the page and become a learning powerhouse!

Part Two: East

SKILL UP

The Lifelong Learner: *Always hungry for knowledge, this curious persona thrives on acquiring new skills and adapting to change. They seamlessly blend traditional education with cutting-edge technology, mastering hard and soft skills.*

FOUR

Becoming Unstoppable

> *In a world where change is the only constant, your ability to learn, unlearn, and relearn will be your greatest asset.*

If you hope to be done with learning once you finish school, you're in for a bit of a surprise. It never stops, but this chapter will show you why!

The best thing about continuous learning is that it will involve something other than exams, essays, or speaking in front of your class! There are many ways to learn, and as you grow into adulthood, there will be numerous opportunities to find content and courses that match your interests and preferred learning style.

In case you wondered if being an eternal student in your industry and life as a whole is relevant, take note of the following:

- 85% of jobs in 2030 have yet to be invented.
- Learning keeps your brain working optimally.
- It helps you stay connected and increases your self-fulfillment.

As Albert Einstein so wisely said, "Once you stop learning, you start dying."

Why Does Learning Never Stop?

Think of all the things your parents and grandparents had to learn as adults that weren't even invented when they were kids—like using smartphones, apps, Zoom calls, and even the Internet! Every new technological wave brings a need to upskill and adapt.

Here are some key reasons why lifelong learning is so vital:

- **Technology is evolving at warp speed.** New technologies are revolutionizing how we work, communicate, and live. Upskilling is crucial to understanding and leveraging these new realms.
- **Career changes are the new norm.** Gone are the days of getting one job and sticking with it for life. The average person changes careers around 3 to 7 times in their lifetime! (The University of Queensland, 2023).
- **Knowledge becomes rapidly outdated.** Continuous learning is the best way to future-proof your career and personal growth.
- **New skills are constantly emerging.** Recent in-demand skills are appearing on the radar, from artificial intelligence, machine learning, and cybersecurity to adaptability, emotional intelligence, and cross-cultural communication. Lifelong learners stay ahead of the curve.

So let this sink in—your learning days are far from over! In fact, they've only just begun. Investing in yourself through continuous upskilling is the best career insurance policy you can have.

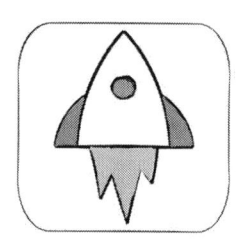

How to Cultivate a Lifelong Learning Mindset

Okay, so you're convinced you need to be a permanent student of life. But how do you actually embrace this lifelong learning mindset? According to UNESCO, four pillars make up lifelong learning:

- **Learn to do:** Do you enjoy picking up new skills? Do you like learning how to do things, like trying a sport, working with a device, or playing an instrument?
- **Learn to be:** Are you always trying to be more creative? Do you look for ways to improve who you are and find fulfillment for yourself? Do you enjoy self-help techniques?

- **Learn to know:** Do you like new information, picking apart things to understand them better? Do you enjoy analyzing details and facts? Do you ask lots of questions?
- **Learn to live together:** Do you look for ways to get along with others better? Are you constantly trying to understand people, practicing tolerance and mutual respect?

If you answered "yes" to any of these questions, congratulations—you're already on your way to being a lifelong learner!

Here are some more essential tips to cultivate this mindset:

- **Stay curious:** Never lose your curiosity about the world around you. Keep exploring new topics and ideas. Take a deep dive into subjects that fascinate you.
- **Embrace challenges:** Don't shy away from steep learning curves —lean into them! Break down complex topics into manageable chunks, and seek help when needed.
- **Reflect and adapt:** You tried out for the school play but didn't get the part. Reflect on your audition—what could you improve next time? Could you take an acting class or practice more to refine your skills? Learn from your successes and failures to improve continuously.
- **Read, read, read:** Expose yourself to diverse perspectives and knowledge through books, articles, and blogs—anything that stretches your mind and introduces new concepts. Audiobooks and podcasts count, too!
- **Incorporate online learning:** Utilize the wealth of online learning opportunities. Bootcamps, courses, interactive apps, YouTube tutorials, and virtual learning hubs are ways to efficiently build new skills and understanding in any subject.
- **Seek inspiration:** Surround yourself with people and experiences that awaken your passion for learning and growth.
- **Set learning goals:** Craft an upskilling plan! Map out the new skills you wish to develop and the knowledge areas you want to explore. Set concrete learning goals to keep you focused.
- **Learn from history:** Understanding history can provide valuable insights and lessons. Studying historical events, cultures, people, and achievements helps you appreciate the present and make informed decisions for the future.
- **Be a student of life:** Approach each day as an opportunity to learn something new, whether it's through conversations, trying

new activities, or simply observing the world with fresh eyes. Life is one big classroom!

By incorporating these practices into your daily life, you'll cultivate a lifelong learning mindset that will serve you well in all your pursuits.

Effective Learning Techniques

Now that you're fired up to be a lifelong learner let's look at some powerful and effective techniques (Cam, 2020):

- **The Feynman Technique:** Named after physicist Richard Feynman, this method helps you develop a deep understanding by simplifying complex topics following these steps:

    - *Step 1:* Learn by teaching.
    - *Step 2:* Explain concepts simply.
    - *Step 3:* Identify knowledge gaps.
    - *Step 4:* Refine your understanding and repeat.

- **Retrieval practice:** Simply re-reading your notes or textbook isn't practical for locking information into your long-term memory. Instead, try actively recalling information through flashcards, quizzes, and summarization.
- **Spaced repetition:** Review material at optimal time intervals for better long-term retention. Our brains hold more information when we review it over extended periods than when we cram it all into one sitting.
- **Learning projects:** Nothing beats on-the-job learning! Apply your knowledge through hands-on projects, internships, or other opportunities.

Developing effective learning methods tailored to the modern age and your lifestyle will ensure that new knowledge and skills are retained and that you create lasting habits.

Embracing Technology

New technologies are transforming our world at lightspeed. Rather than feeling intimidated, embrace these innovations and upskill to leverage them effectively.

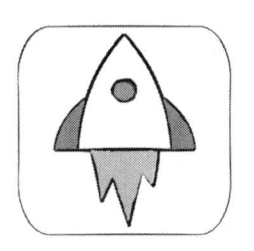

Think about the first time you drove a car. It likely felt confusing and nerve-wracking at first. But once you spent some time with it, you realized it was pretty user-friendly and made your life so much easier in many ways; for starters, it gave you wings!

The same applies to emerging technologies like artificial intelligence, virtual reality, and blockchain.

By pushing yourself to learn new things in your learning style, you can begin to enjoy and understand things even more. And remember, if you learn to sing, it doesn't mean you must become a singer. You are simply wiring your brain to be open to new possibilities and skills.

To stay ahead, here are some essential tech-era skills to develop:

Digital Literacy

Digital literacy is the cornerstone of modern life and work.

It encompasses the ability to navigate, evaluate, and create content using digital technologies. This includes mastering productivity tools like Microsoft Office or Google Workspace, understanding data privacy and online security, and effectively communicating across various digital platforms.

It also involves media literacy—critically analyzing online information and identifying misinformation.

As our world becomes increasingly digital, these skills are crucial for academic success, career advancement, and informed citizenship. Developing strong digital literacy empowers you to harness technology's full potential while navigating its challenges responsibly.

Artificial Intelligence and Large Language Models

The rise of AI and large language models (LLMs) is revolutionizing how we interact with technology. These tools can assist with writing, coding, research, design, and problem-solving. While powerful, they require human guidance to be truly effective.

Develop skills in:

- Prompt engineering to effectively communicate with these systems
- Critical evaluation of AI-generated content
- Understanding their capabilities and limitations
- Ethical considerations in their use

By embracing these technologies responsibly, you can enhance your productivity and creativity while staying ahead in an AI-driven world.

Analytical Skills

Learn coding, data analysis, and critical thinking to make data-driven decisions. This skill set is becoming increasingly valuable as businesses rely on data to drive strategy. Key areas include (Simplilearn 2024):

- **Coding:** Understanding programming languages like Python, Java, or SQL allows you to automate tasks, analyze large data sets, and build web applications.
- **Data analysis:** Using tools like Excel or Tableau to visualize and draw insights from data is a highly sought-after skill in many industries.
- **Critical thinking:** The ability to logically break down complex problems, evaluate arguments, and make reasoned judgments is essential in any role.
- **Quantitative reasoning:** The ability to handle numerical data, perform calculations, and understand quantitative methods. This skill is of great importance, especially in numbers-related fields like engineering and finance.
- **Research:** These skills involve gathering data from numerous sources, obtaining the most helpful information, and using it effectively. This skill is valuable in multiple professions, including writing, science, and law.

- **Attention to detail:** A vital skill for ensuring accurate work. Attention to detail is critical in almost every profession as it enables you to confirm your work does not contain potentially costly mistakes.
- **Strategic thinking:** If you plan on making it big in business or sales, strategic thinking is a skill to prioritize. Being a good strategist is particularly vital if you plan on managing a company or holding an executive position.

Innovation Mindset

As the world rapidly evolves, the ability to think outside the box and develop original ideas and solutions is becoming a key differentiator. An innovation mindset embraces:

- **Creativity:** The ability to generate novel concepts, make unexpected connections, and approach problems from fresh angles.
- **Problem-solving:** Skills in brainstorming, prototyping, and testing solutions to complex challenges.
- **Collaboration:** The ability to work effectively in diverse teams, communicate ideas, and build on others' strengths.

Staying Curious and Adaptable

With the pace of innovation today, simply reacting to change is no longer enough. You must anticipate emerging trends and proactively upskill to stay ahead of the curve. In fact, adaptability isn't just a nice-to-have skill; it's become a critical requirement for success in the modern workplace.

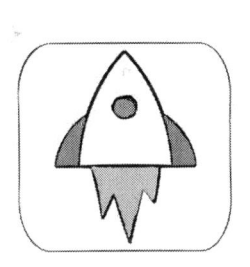

Consider these eye-opening statistics:

- 58% of the workforce will need new skills to do their jobs successfully (Gartner, 2021).
- 44% of workers' skills will be disrupted in the next five years (The World Economic Forum, 2023)
- 91% of companies say they must change their organizational model to be more adaptable (Mercer, 2021).

These numbers underscore a crucial point: the ability to adapt and learn continuously is now essential for long-term career success.

Here's how you can cultivate this mindset:

- **Build your radar:** Follow influencers, thought leaders, and credible publications in your areas of passion and interest. This will help you spot new ideas, forecasts, and innovations before they become mainstream.
- **Be an early adopter:** Watch for new platforms, tools, and technologies making waves. Doing so will expose you to these breakthroughs sooner and accelerate your learning curve. Volunteer for work or school pilot projects involving new technologies or methodologies.
- **Learn in-demand skills:** Regularly read forecasting reports and job market analysis to identify high-demand skills in 5 to 10 years. Build a roadmap to acquire them.
- **Create, don't just consume:** While reading and digesting information is excellent, real learning happens when you put that knowledge into practice. Challenge yourself by creating practical outputs like blogs, videos, apps, or products based on what you're learning. This hands-on approach reinforces your learning and builds a portfolio of work that can showcase your creativity and adaptability to potential employers.

By cultivating a spirit of curiosity and adaptability, you'll be equipped to pivot and thrive no matter how rapidly the world evolves around you.

Balancing Technology Use

Excessive screen time can lead to physical, mental, and social challenges, such as eye strain, sleep disruption, digital addiction, and reduced face-to-face interaction. Studies have shown that it is linked to depression. Undoubtedly, smartphones and other devices are part of daily life for most people. Still, it is crucial to maintain a healthy balance between online and real-life experiences.

It's also vital to be a savvy tech user and know that some apps and platforms are designed to hook you, primarily gaming and social media. Every reward in a game, a "like" on social media, or a "ping" in chats produces serotonin (a feel-good chemical) in your body, causing a dependency—just like a drug (Siler 2024). As much as you want to stop, you just can't until functioning without your phone causes anxiety and stress.

Tech-Health Check

Nomophobia, the fear of being without access to a working cell phone, is on the rise. Take the nomophobia quiz to assess your smartphone dependence. You simply need to agree or disagree and keep track of your answers.

1. My smartphone is the first thing I look at when I wake up and the last thing I look at before I go to sleep.
2. My smartphone goes everywhere with me.
3. Nobody is allowed to touch my smartphone except me.
4. I would rather chat on my smartphone than talk to my friends in person.
5. I'm jealous because my friend has a newer smartphone.
6. I'm never bored, thanks to my smartphone.
7. It is rude of people to expect me to stop looking at my smartphone just because they're talking to me.
8. I can only sit through a 2-hour film at the movies if I check my smartphone multiple times.
9. My phone is almost an extension of my hand.
10. My blue light glasses are part of my fashion now.
11. People often tell me that I'm addicted to my smartphone.
12. I love my smartphone.

Scoring and Interpretation

Count the number of statements you agreed with:

0–3: You have a healthy relationship with your smartphone and are not likely to have nomophobia.

4–6: You have a moderate dependence on your smartphone and may be at risk of developing nomophobia. Consider implementing strategies to reduce your reliance on your device.

7–9: You have a significant dependence on your smartphone and are likely experiencing symptoms of nomophobia. It's critical to establish a healthier balance with your device.

10–12: You have a severe dependence on your smartphone and are highly likely to have nomophobia. It's crucial to seek help and implement strategies to reduce reliance on your device and improve your overall well-being.

Strategies for a Healthy Digital Balance

Implement the following strategies for a healthy digital balance:

- **Establish device-free zones.** Create spaces where phones and devices are out of reach, such as at the dinner table or riding the car with friends. This encourages more meaningful conversations and allows you to be fully present in the moment.
- **Practice mindful ignoring.** When you're engaged in an important task or in the middle of a conversation, resist the urge to check your phone every time it pings. Train your willpower by turning off notifications during specific activities and prioritizing your focus and productivity.
- **Use grayscale mode.** Change your mobile phone settings to grayscale to reduce glare and the attraction of intense colors. This simple strategy can help minimize the compulsion to check your phone frequently. It can make it easier to focus on other tasks.
- **Prioritize sleep.** Avoid using your phone as an alarm clock, as it can tempt you to check it during the night. Aim for at least one to two hours of screen-free before bed to help your brain wind down.
- **Set limits and be accountable.** Establish reasonable time limits for device use. Utilize built-in screen time tracking features on your phone to monitor your usage and set goals. Reward yourself for meeting those goals and take regular breaks to engage in offline activities.
- **Embrace transparency.** While privacy is important, being open about Internet usage can help you resist temptation. Use devices in shared spaces where others can hold you accountable. Would you feel comfortable watching, saying, or doing the things you currently engage online in front of others?
- **Beware of predators.** The internet can be a hunting ground for those with malicious intent. Be cautious about sharing personal information online and meeting people you've only interacted

with virtually. Be aware of the dangers of pornography, which can distort perceptions of relationships and sexuality. Learn to recognize grooming behaviors and report suspicious activities to trusted adults or authorities. Your safety and well-being should always be your top priority in the digital world!
- **Engage in offline hobbies.** Pursue interests that don't involve screens. Prioritize socializing and engaging with people face-to-face.

Balancing technology in life is tricky. You want to stay updated with the latest trends and use technology to unlock your learning potential. Still, you don't want to become addicted to or manipulated by your devices. When you're in control of your phone rather than vice versa, you truly experience the freedom and power of technology.

The Takeaway

In a world where technology is advancing at breakneck speed, adopting a lifelong learning mindset is no longer optional—it's essential. Remember, learning is not a destination but a journey that will enrich your life in countless ways. So, embrace the adventure and never stop growing!

To truly thrive in today's fast-paced, interconnected world, you'll also need to develop an arsenal of essential life skills—so get ready to take your skill set to the next level and unleash your full potential. The power-ups await!

FIVE

Powering Up Your Soft Skills

> *Soft skills get little respect but will make or break your career.*
>
> Peggy Klaus

In an era of constant change and global connectivity, it's not just about what you know but how effectively you apply that knowledge and interact with others. This is where the power of soft skills comes into play.

While hard skills are the technical abilities specific to a job or task, soft skills are the personal attributes that enable you to navigate your environment, work well with others, and achieve your goals.

Hard skills are typically quantifiable and teachable, such as data analysis, proficiency in a foreign language, graphic design, algebra, biology, writing, editing, cooking, and teaching. You get it, right? These skills are often the focus of traditional education and training programs.

Soft skills, on the other hand, encompass a wide range of interpersonal and intrapersonal competencies. Some examples include empathy, adaptability, good listening, leadership, organization, integrity, reliability, time management, punctuality, teamwork, and knowing how to resolve problems effectively.

The importance of soft skills cannot be overstated. According to LinkedIn's Global Talent Trends report, 92% of hiring professionals consider soft skills equally or more important than hard skills. Moreover, 89% believe a lack of critical soft skills is the top reason for new hire failures (Manrique, 2024).

So, it's time to power up your soft skills to help you adapt to changing environments, stand out in any field you pursue, and become the best version of yourself.

This chapter will explore essential soft skills and provide practical strategies to help you cultivate these powerful attributes.

Let's dive in and discover what they are.

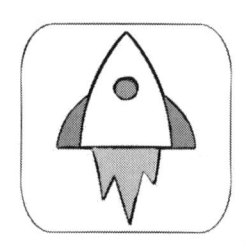

Priorities: Rock Your To-Do List

How often have you spent hours scrolling through social media or binge-watching a show, only to realize you forgot to study for that big test or work on your college applications? It's easy to get caught up in distractions and lose sight of what matters most.

You might be overwhelmed with a never-ending to-do list and need help figuring out where to start.

This is where the power of prioritization comes in. As Stephen Covey wisely said, "The key is not to prioritize what's on your schedule, but to schedule your priorities." Let's explore how you can master this essential skill and ensure the most important tasks get the time and energy they deserve.

- **Start with your values.** Remember those core values we talked about in Chapter One? Use them as your compass for setting priorities. If one of your top values is family, for example, then make sure you're carving out quality time with your loved ones, even if it means saying no to watching the latest episode of your favorite show.
- **Set SMART goals.** When you're deciding what to prioritize, it helps to get specific. Set goals that are:

- **S**—Specific
- **M**—Measurable
- **A**—Achievable
- **R**—Relevant
- **T**—Timely

So instead of saying, "I want to apply for college," try something like, "I will submit five college applications by September 15th." This way, you know exactly what you aim for and can track your progress and adjust as needed.

- **Use the 80/20 rule.** This is the idea that 80% of your results often come from just 20% of your efforts. In other words, focus on the few things that will move the needle. Imagine drowning in college brochures, thinking you must apply to every school under the sun. Instead of burning out on 30 applications (and draining your wallet in the process), why not pick your top 6 schools that tick all your boxes (roughly 20% of 30) and pour your heart and soul into those applications.
- **Try the Eisenhower Matrix.** This is a handy tool for categorizing your tasks based on urgency and importance. Draw a square and divide it into four boxes:

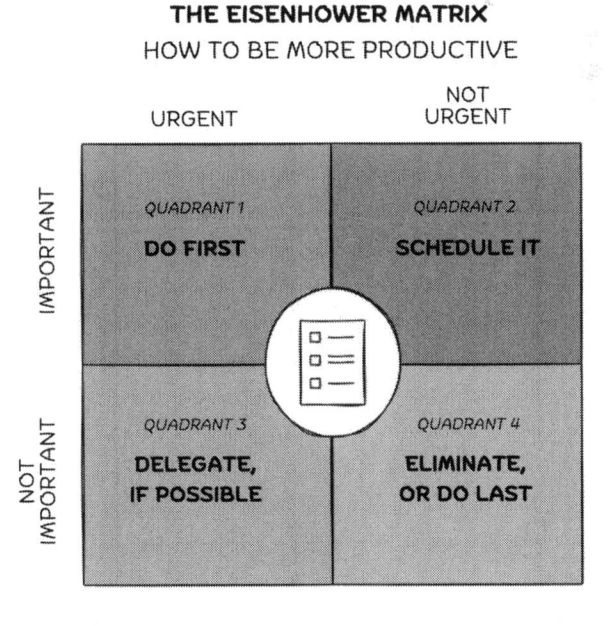

THE EISENHOWER MATRIX
HOW TO BE MORE PRODUCTIVE

	URGENT	NOT URGENT
IMPORTANT	QUADRANT 1 DO FIRST	QUADRANT 2 SCHEDULE IT
NOT IMPORTANT	QUADRANT 3 DELEGATE, IF POSSIBLE	QUADRANT 4 ELIMINATE, OR DO LAST

○ *Urgent and Important:* This is your VIP list. Do these tasks first. For example, study for tomorrow's test.

○ *Important but Not Urgent:* Schedule these for later. The future you will thank you! For example, research potential colleges and programs.

○ *Urgent but Not Important:* Share the load—delegate if possible. For example, taking your work clothes to the laundry. Ask your sister or mom to cover for you, but don't abuse their generosity! Next time, plan accordingly.

○ *Neither Urgent nor Important:* Trash these tasks or do them at the end, such as getting your nails done.

The more you practice these techniques, the easier prioritizing will become. And, trust me, it's a skill that will serve you well in all areas of life—from passing your exams with flying colors to landing your dream job or planning an epic adventure with your friends.

So next time you feel overwhelmed by everything on your plate, step back and ask yourself: "What's really important here?" "What aligns with my values and goals?" Focus on those things first and let the rest fall into place. You've got this!

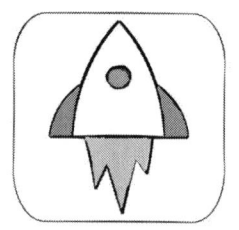

Setting Boundaries: The Art of Saying No

All right, let's talk about the art of saying no. I know, I know, it might sound counterintuitive—aren't we supposed to say yes to every opportunity that comes our way? Well, not exactly.

You see? Setting boundaries is like being the bouncer of your own life. Like a bouncer decides who gets into the party, you can decide what you let into your schedule. And sometimes, that means saying no to things that don't align with your values and priorities.

And speaking of boundaries, they can take many forms, including: (Martin 2020)

- **Physical boundaries:** You decide the boundaries you set for your body and the space you need. For instance, you choose whether you are okay with being hugged.
- **Material boundaries:** You decide what you wish to spend your money on and whether you are okay with lending clothing, for example.

- **Belief boundaries:** You have a right to your beliefs. For example, political, moral, or spiritual issues cannot be imposed on you. Those are very personal.
- **Sexual boundaries:** You decide what you consent to or not.
- **Intellectual boundaries:** You have a right to think your own thoughts and have different opinions.
- **Emotional boundaries:** You have a right to feel the emotions you do.
- **Time boundaries:** You decide how you spend your time.

Boundaries can be flexible or non-negotiable, depending on the situation and your values.

- **Non-negotiable boundaries** are essential, and you need them to feel safe. A non-negotiable boundary might be refusing to try a drug or compromising your academic integrity by cheating on a test.
- A more **flexible boundary** could arise when you've set aside focused study time and turned off notifications. Still, a friend calls your home phone because they're experiencing a personal crisis and need support. In this case, you might briefly step away from your studies to offer comfort, demonstrating the importance of balancing your commitments with compassion for others.

So, how can you start practicing the art of saying no? Here are a few tips:

- **Be honest and direct.** Don't make excuses or beat around the bush.
- **Offer an alternative if possible.** If you can't attend an event, suggest another time to catch up.
- **Remember, "No" is a complete sentence.** You don't always have to explain yourself.
- **Be confident in your decision.** You're not being selfish—you're being smart.
- **Start using the phrase "I don't."** It allows you to avoid making excuses for things you don't want to do. For instance, you can tell your friends, "Sorry, I don't do drugs." And that is the end of the conversation. You'll be respected for that.

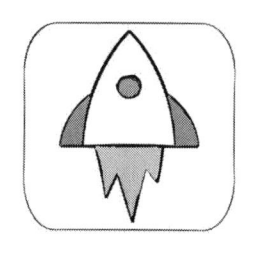

Time Management: Time Is Gold!

Alissa checked her phone, not for messages, but for the time. She was working out if she would make it off the bus, down to the changing rooms, get her kit on, and be on the field in less than ten minutes. Her coach had warned her that she might get kicked off the team if she was late again. Hanging out with her friends after school was important; her friends meant the world to her! But as she rechecked her phone, she wished she had left just a few minutes earlier.

Let's talk about the golden resource we wish we had more: time. It's one of the only things we can't buy, store, or get back once it's gone, so learning to manage your time like a boss is essential.

Think about it: how often have you found yourself rushing, like Alissa, to finish a project at the last minute or showing up late to an appointment because you got sidetracked or did not allocate enough time? It's a stressful feeling, right? But here's the thing: with some planning and innovative strategies, you can control your time and make every moment count.

Remember how we talked about setting priorities and boundaries? Well, effective time management ties right into that. When you know what's most important to you, deciding how to allocate your time is straightforward. And when you can say no to things that don't align with your goals, you free up more space for the things that do.

But how do you manage your time effectively? Use these techniques:

- **Create a schedule.** List your commitments, deadlines, and goals at the beginning of each week. Be realistic about how long tasks will take. Remember to include time for nurturing relationships, self-care, and relaxation.
- **Use time-blocking.** This is where you dedicate specific chunks of time to particular activities. For example, you might block off 9–11 a.m. for working on a project, 12–1 p.m. for lunch and exercise, and 2–4 p.m. for focus work like studying. The key is to focus solely on the task at hand during each block without getting distracted by other things. Yes, also set some time apart for goofing around and socializing.

A word of caution: These are tools to help you get organized and manage your time better, not a rigid prison. Don't stress if your schedule doesn't go as planned – it usually doesn't! Remember, you can still control your time and adjust as needed.

When planning your schedule, consider these common pitfalls in time management:

- Underestimating task duration
- Failing to account for unexpected interruptions
- Not considering energy levels throughout the day
- Overcommitting or saying "yes" too often
- Procrastination due to perfectionism or fear of failure
- Neglecting to schedule breaks or downtime
- Allowing distractions like social media to derail focus
- Not adapting the schedule when priorities shift

Recognizing these challenges can help you create more realistic and practical schedules.

So, go forth and conquer your calendar! You'll be amazed at how much you can accomplish with planning and thoughtful strategies.

Productivity: Moving the Needle

Now that you've got a handle on setting priorities, boundaries, and time management, let's put it together and discuss a next-level strategy to help you crush it!

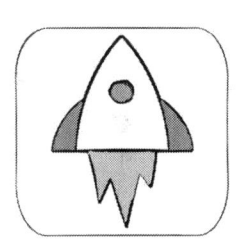

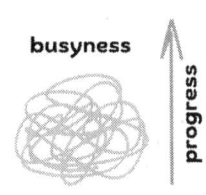

Productivity is efficiently converting your time and effort into meaningful results. It's not just about being busy; it's about making progress toward your goals.

Effective productivity ties directly into planning. When you plan well, you set yourself up for productive action.

Here are two powerful strategies to boost your productivity:

The Ivy Lee Method

This simple but incredibly effective technique helps you plan, prioritize, and focus on one task at a time instead of trying to juggle a million things at once. Here's how it works (Clear, n.d.):

- At the day's end, list tomorrow's six most important tasks. Be specific and realistic—don't bite off more than you can chew!
- Rank these tasks by importance.
- The next day, start with the top task and work until it's done. No multitasking allowed!
- Move on to the next task, repeating the process.
- At the day's end, move any unfinished tasks to tomorrow's list.
- Repeat daily.

Limit yourself to six daily tasks to maintain focus and avoid overwhelm.

The Pomodoro Technique

This method is excellent for focused work! It breaks work into dedicated intervals:

- Choose a task to work on.
- Set a timer for 25 minutes (one "Pomodoro").
- Work on the task until the timer rings.
- Take a 5-minute break to stretch, grab a snack, or relax.
- After four Pomodoros, reward yourself with a more extended 15 to 30-minute break.

This technique helps maintain concentration, manages mental fatigue, and creates a sense of urgency to complete tasks efficiently. You'll be amazed at how much you can accomplish in two hours!

By implementing these strategies, you'll accomplish more in less time. Remember, productivity isn't about perfection but progress in the right direction. Experiment with these methods and adapt them to fit your style and needs. With practice, you'll develop a productivity system that works best for you, helping you achieve your goals more efficiently and effectively.

Overcoming Productivity Zappers

Now, let's examine the enemies of productivity: procrastination, distractions, multitasking, and low energy.

Procrastination

Let's talk about procrastination, the enemy of productivity. We've all been there—you know you need to do something, but you just can't seem to get started. Did you know that 50% of college students procrastinate chronically, and up to 95% do so at some point?

Procrastination doesn't just stop you from getting things done; it increases your stress levels and prevents you from achieving optimal academic and work performance (Shatz, n.d.). Ultimately, you must accomplish the task with stress and tension or on your own time and with peace of mind. Which one makes more sense?

People procrastinate for many reasons, including lack of motivation, low self-confidence, and anxiety. Sometimes, procrastination occurs because you think you have more time left to do a task than it takes. The two-minute rule is the perfect antidote to this problem.

The Two-Minute Rule

The simple yet powerful rule states that if you can complete a task in two minutes or fewer, do it right now instead of postponing or scheduling it.

The real power of the two-minute rule lies in its ability to overcome inertia and kick-start your productivity. Here's how it works:

- Focusing on tasks that take just two minutes lowers the barrier to getting started. It feels manageable and non-threatening.
- Once you start a task, you will likely continue beyond the initial two minutes. This phenomenon is known as task momentum or the Zeigarnik effect—our brains naturally want to complete what we've begun.
- Even if you only do the two-minute version of a larger task, you've still made progress. This progress, however small, can motivate you to return to the task later and do more.

- Completing these small tasks gives you a sense of accomplishment, boosting your mood and confidence. This positive reinforcement makes you more likely to tackle more significant tasks.
- By quickly addressing small tasks, you declutter your mind and to-do list, allowing you to focus better on larger, more time-consuming projects.

Nearly any habit can be scaled down into a two-minute starting point. For example (Baffert, 2021):

- Instead of "reading for an hour," start with "read one page."
- Instead of "going for a run," begin with "put on my running shoes."
- Instead of "writing a paper," start with "open a new document and write one sentence."
- Instead of "doing laundry," begin with "separate colors and whites."

The point is to make getting started so easy that you can't possibly procrastinate. Break down big tasks into smaller chunks. And once you start, chances are you'll keep going and make real progress on your task.

So next time you procrastinate, ask yourself: "What's my two-minute starting point?" Then dive in and watch your productivity soar!

Distractions

In our hyper-connected world, distractions are everywhere, threatening to derail our focus and productivity. Technology, social media, or a crowded room can be huge distractions. However, you have the power to take control. Here are some strategies to help you minimize distractions and stay on track:

- Make a "To-Do" list so you stay focused.
- Turn off the TV and other noisy distractions.
- Use music and headphones to drown out noise if this helps you concentrate.
- Silence alerts and notifications, and put your phone away.
- Set times for you to only respond to text messages during breaks.
- Ensure your desk or workspace is clean and well-organized.
- Close your door or hang a "Focused Time" sign at your door.

By implementing these strategies, you can create an environment conducive to focus and productivity, allowing you to accomplish more in less time.

Multitasking

Research shows that multitasking makes us less productive because it distracts us, slows us down, and impairs our ability to determine how, when, and in what order tasks are fulfilled (Cherry, 2023). Instead, give your full attention to one task at a time. You'll work more efficiently and produce better results. To break the multitasking habit:

- Limit the number of tasks you set out to accomplish to one at a time.
- Tackle big tasks first so you feel accomplished when you complete them.
- Use the Pomodoro technique, as mentioned above, for focused work.
- Batch similar tasks together.
- Practice mindfulness to help you recognize when you're multitasking.

Remember to use the productivity tools suggested in this book to support your well-being, not as a means to push yourself to the point of burnout. Be mindful of your own limits, and make sure to prioritize self-care alongside your productivity goals.

Low Energy

Feeling emotionally or physically drained can significantly impact your productivity. When your energy is low, tasks that generally seem manageable can feel overwhelming, and your ability to focus and make decisions can suffer. This can lead to procrastination, decreased quality of work, and increased stress.

To combat low energy and maintain productivity:

- Prioritize sleep and maintain a consistent sleep schedule.
- Practice good nutrition habits, focusing on balanced meals and staying hydrated.
- Incorporate regular exercise into your routine, even if it's just a short walk.

- Take short breaks throughout the day to recharge.
- Use the Pomodoro Technique to manage your energy in focused bursts.
- Practice stress-management techniques like deep breathing or meditation.
- Identify your most productive hours and schedule essential tasks accordingly.

Managing your energy is just as important as managing your time. In later chapters, we'll delve deeper into strategies for boosting your physical and emotional well-being, providing you with a comprehensive toolkit for maintaining high energy and productivity.

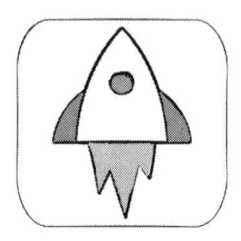

Communication: Much More than Saying It Right!

> *Did you know which is the most powerful muscle in your body? It's not the quads. It's not the jaw. It's the tongue! The tongue has the power to destroy a person's reputation or self-esteem. But it also has the power to uplift and encourage! Which one do you choose?*

Let's discuss the superpower that can make or break just about any situation in life: effective communication. Whether you're trying to set boundaries, manage your time, lead a team, or engage in everyday interactions, how you communicate can be the difference between success and a total mess.

So, what does it mean to communicate effectively? It's not just about being clear and concise, although that's certainly part of it. Effective communication is also about attitude: being empathetic, open-minded, and adaptable to your audience.

Think about it: you wouldn't talk to your grandma like you talk to your best friend, right? Different audiences have different needs, knowledge levels, and communication styles. Tailor your message accordingly.

Let's dig into the essence of excellent communication, then!

Communication Techniques That Work

Communication doesn't just involve what you say; it includes body language, texting or writing style, and how you listen. Good communication is clear, correct, complete, concise, compassionate, and two-way. Here's how to do it right:

- **Watch nonverbal cues:** Nonverbal cues like body language, facial expressions, and tone of voice can speak volumes. In fact, 93% of communication is nonverbal, with body language contributing 55% and tone of voice 38%. In comparison, words only account for 7% of the message (Mehrabian, 1981).

For example, crossing your arms and avoiding eye contact can make you seem closed off and defensive, even if that's not your intention. On the other hand, maintaining an open posture and a friendly tone can make others feel more at ease and receptive to your message.

- **Active listening:** This technique involves fully concentrating on the speaker, understanding their message, and responding thoughtfully.

Example: Your friend is telling you about a fight with their parents. Instead of immediately jumping in with your opinion, try this:

  - *Put away distractions (like your phone).*
  - *Make eye contact and nod to show you're listening.*
  - *Ask clarifying questions: "How did that make you feel?"*
  - *Paraphrase what they've said: "So if I understand correctly, you're upset because..."*
  - *Showing you care about what they say through phrases like, "I get you," "That must be tough," and "Yes, I can see that."*
  - *Don't interrupt.*
  - *Don't wait for a conversation gap to inject your thoughts quickly. Be patient!*

- **Practice empathy:** Try to understand the other person's perspective.

Scenario: "Your friend is upset because he didn't make the school sports team. But you did! Instead of jumping and celebrating in front of him, dismissing his feelings, you could reach out and put yourself in his shoes and offer words of encouragement."

- **Control your emotions:** Count to ten before responding, especially in heated situations. If emotions run high, postponing the conversation for a few hours or days can be better.

Scenario: Your sibling accuses you of taking their favorite shirt without asking. Your first impulse might be to lash out defensively. Instead, take a deep breath, count to ten, and respond calmly: "I understand you're upset. Let's look for your shirt together, and if I did take it by mistake, I'll apologize."

- **Use "I" statements:** This technique helps express your feelings without blaming others.

Example: Instead of saying, "You never listen to me," try: "I feel frustrated when I'm speaking and don't feel heard."

- **Be clear and concise:** Express your thoughts in a focused, organized manner, avoiding jargon or filler words.

Example: Instead of saying, "Um, I was thinking that maybe, if it's okay with you, we could possibly, like, study together for the test next week or whatever," try: "Would you like to study together for next week's test?"

- **Know your audience**: Before you start communicating, take a moment to consider who you're talking to and what they need from you. Are you speaking to a friend, a teacher, or a potential employer? Tailor your message accordingly.

Scenario: You're explaining why you need a new laptop. To your tech-savvy friend, you might say: "My current processor can't handle the new software I need for my coding class." To your grandparents, you might say: "My current computer is too slow to do my schoolwork efficiently."

- **Be culturally sensitive:** In today's globalized world, developing an awareness of different communication styles and norms across cultures is essential. Take the time to learn about the cultural background of the person you're communicating with. Be open to adapting your style to ensure your message is understood and well-received.
- **Give and receive feedback gracefully:** Learn to give constructive criticism and accept feedback without getting defensive.

- **Practice, practice, practice:** Seek opportunities to speak in public, write for different audiences, or engage in difficult conversations to build your communication muscles.

Saying It Online

Texting and social media are great for connecting with friends and out-of-town relatives. Still, they can cause misunderstandings if handled poorly. Here are some tips for better online communication:

- Take your time to write. Check before you send (read twice).
- Read more than you type.
- Keep emotions out! If emotions are high, wait a few hours to calm down before pressing "send."
- Don't use ALL CAPS. Avoid sarcasm.
- Know when to group chat and private message.
- Be selective and think about what to broadcast to the world, if anything at all.
- Be friendly and kind; nasty can come back to bite you.

The golden rule of online communication is to say it as if the person is right in front of you, looking into your eyes. This approach ensures you remain respectful and empathetic, fostering stronger relationships and avoiding misunderstandings.

Remember, effective communication is a skill that improves with practice. Implementing these techniques in daily interactions will build stronger relationships, avoid misunderstandings, and express yourself more confidently. There's always room to grow and improve your communication skills.

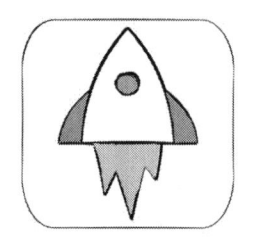

Leadership: Walk Your Talk

One thing is communicating effectively, and another is backing your words and message with your actions!

Leadership isn't just about being the boss or having a fancy title. It's about inspiring and guiding others toward a common goal, whether you're working on a school project, organizing an event, or even just helping your family plan a vacation.

Even if you don't think of yourself as a leader, you probably already influence others more than you realize. Sociologists say that even the most isolated person will influence 10,000 others in their lifetime. That's a lot of power!

Leadership Qualities

So, what makes a great leader? Effective leadership starts with the right attitude and mindset to positively influence others. The best leaders have certain qualities, almost like an invisible magnet, that inspire others to naturally follow them. Let's break it down:

- **Authenticity:** Remember when we talked about self-awareness in Chapter One? Knowing who you are and acting in alignment with your true self. That's the key to being an authentic leader. Don't try to be someone you're not—just be the best version of yourself.
- **Empathy:** Great leaders care about people. They put themselves in others' shoes and try to understand their perspective. For instance, when a friend struggles with a challenging situation at home, an empathetic leader listens to them, offers support, and helps them find a solution.
- **Humility:** A great leader serves others, not themselves. They put others first and focus on building the group as a whole. They don't try to be the center of attention; they help highlight the talents and abilities of their group or team.
- **Integrity:** Leaders stay true to their values, even when it's hard. They make decisions based on their principles, not just what's popular. They lead by example, not just by telling others what to do. They show them how.
- **Adaptability:** The world is constantly changing, and great leaders know how to roll with the punches. They're always learning and

growing. Great leaders stay calm and adapt to new situations without freaking out.
- **Communication:** Effective leaders are masters of both speaking and listening. They express their thoughts clearly and kindly while valuing others' ideas and opinions.

A prime example of the power of effective communication in leadership is Mr. Smith, my son's fourth-grade teacher. During a rowdy field trip, instead of shouting over the noise, he stood silently with crossed arms and, in a calm, quiet voice, said only once, "Kids, it's time to sit down and pay attention." Remarkably, within minutes, the entire group was seated and attentive. This experience highlighted two crucial lessons: leaders don't need to be the loudest voice in the room, and respect and kindness are powerful leadership tools.

- **Influence:** Ultimately, leaders inspire others to work together toward a common goal. As stated before, leadership is about having the right attitude and mindset to positively influence others. They know how to motivate people and bring out the best in them.

I encourage you to re-read the leadership qualities listed above and, as you read through again, think if you or some of the people in your life embody one or several of these characteristics.

So, how can you start developing your leadership skills? Here are a few ideas:

- Authentically embrace the leadership qualities discussed above.
- Observe and learn from leaders you admire. What makes them effective?
- Continuously work on your communication and emotional intelligence.
- Regularly reflect on your actions and decisions to ensure they align with your values. Do you stay true to yourself?
- Seek out leadership opportunities.
- Be open to feedback and always strive for improvement.

What you say and how you act influence the people you interact with every day. Leadership is another skill in your toolbox that can help you grow and thrive. At school, work, or in your everyday relationships and life.

Skill Booster

Lifelong learning is an ongoing journey. Use these tools regularly to refine your understanding and sharpen your skills.

Embrace Technology

- Create a professional LinkedIn profile and engage with industry leaders in your field of interest. This will showcase your digital communication skills and help you build a solid online presence.
- Test your knowledge and expand your analytical skills by learning advanced Excel techniques online.
- Participate in a hackathon or innovation challenge where you collaborate with a team to develop an original solution to a real-world problem, like designing an app to promote mental health.

Reflect and Plan

- Which skill resonates with you the most, and why?
- What's one specific action you can take this week to start developing that power-up?
- How do you envision these power-ups helping you achieve your personal and professional goals?
- Reflect on one skill that you've always wanted to master. What's holding you back? What first step could you take this week to start learning it?

Skill Development Challenges

- Set a 30-day challenge to learn a new skill or improve an existing one.
- Find an accountability partner to share progress and motivate each other.
- Create a skill swap with a friend – teach each other something you're good at.

Journal Prompts

- What new skill did I learn or practice today?
- How can I apply a skill I already have in a new way?
- What skill do I need to develop to achieve my next goal?

Expand Your Skill Booster Toolkit

Ready to power up? Scan the QR code below to access bonus resources, including videos, recommended tools and apps, and extra tips to embrace lifelong learning and power up your hard and soft skills. Check back often for updates and fresh content.

Power Up Your Game

You've explored the power of lifelong learning, embraced technology, and discovered essential soft skills that will set you apart in any situation. These skills are your toolkit for success in an ever-changing world. Keep pushing yourself to learn and improve as you continue to grow and adapt.

Now, let's shift gears and focus on another crucial aspect of your journey: relationships. In the next part, we'll dive into practical techniques for attracting the right people into your life and building a circle of trust. These connections will be instrumental in supporting your growth and helping you navigate life's challenges. Ready to level up your social game? Let's go!

Help Others Find the Courage to Be Their Most Authentic Selves

Like a stone tossed into a pond, a simple act of kindness creates ripples that reach far beyond what we can see.

Dear Reader,

Your journey through these pages is unique, and your insights could inspire others. If this book has helped you embrace your authentic self, consider sharing your experience.

We'd love to see how you're using *Game-Changing Life Skills for Teens* in your daily life. Leave a review on Amazon with a photo or video showcasing your favorite section, the book's beautiful imagery, or your favorite resource you found via the QR code provided at the end of last chapter. Your visual story could be the spark someone else needs to begin their own journey of self-discovery.

Remember, every step forward, no matter how small, is progress. By sharing your thoughts, you're not just leaving a review – you're extending a hand to others who may be searching for guidance.

Let's create a community of support and inspiration. By leaving a review of this book on Amazon, you'll point new readers to a handy resource that will inspire them to build their lives around their values and passions.

Thank you for being part of this journey. May this book continue to be a source of strength as you lead your most authentic life.

Angela Abraham

SCAN ME

Part Three: South

CIRCLE OF TRUST

The Relationship Navigator:
This character excels at building and maintaining healthy connections. They navigate the complex world of human relationships with empathy, emotional intelligence, and wisdom. They understand the delicate balance of give-and-take, creating a supportive network that withstands life's storms.

SIX

Building Meaningful Connections

> *You are the average of the five people you spend the most time with.*
>
> Jim Rohn

Time is one of our most precious resources. But as Leo Christopher said, "There's only one thing more precious than our time, and that's who we spend it with." This truth underscores how social circles profoundly shape our lives, experiences, and personal growth.

Research shows that our relationships evolve dramatically throughout our lives. A study by Our World in Data reveals a fascinating pattern in how Americans spend their time across different age groups.

Time Spent With Relationships by Age

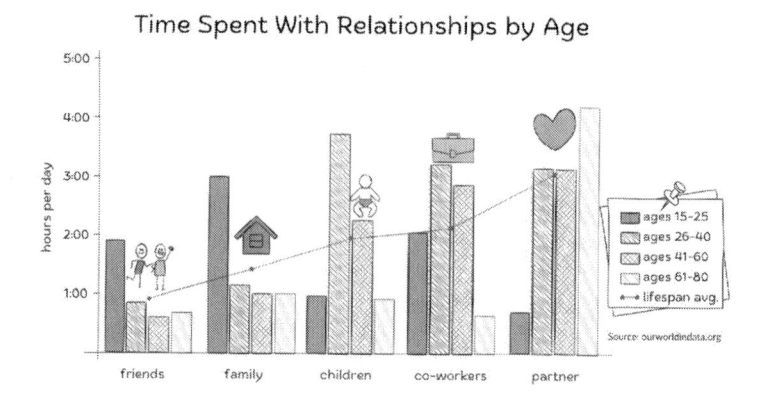

(Chart showing hours per day spent with friends, family, children, co-workers, and partner across ages 15-25, 26-40, 41-60, 61-80, and lifespan avg. Source: ourworldindata.org)

In our early years, we primarily interact with our parents and siblings. As we enter our teens and twenties, time with friends becomes dominant. Later in life, our focus shifts to that special someone, children, and coworkers.

This evolution isn't just about changing preferences; it reflects the powerful influence that different relationships have on us at various life stages. The people around us act as mirrors, mentors, and molders of our character. They challenge our ideas, support our dreams, and sometimes push us in unexpected directions.

Take a moment to reflect on your own social circle. Who are the key players in your life right now? Consider your friends, parents, siblings, mentors, and anyone else. Now, ask yourself:

- Does your time with others align with your core values and goals?
- Are there relationships you neglect or consume too much of your time?
- Is the time you spend with others quality and truly enriching your life?

Ready to map out your relationship landscape and make it work for you? Let's dive in!

The Hunger to Belong

Ever felt like you're alone on this planet? Like you just don't fit in anywhere? That tension in your chest, that longing for connection. We've all been there.

We, humans, are wired to belong—to be part of a tribe, a family, a group, or a community. When you don't feel connected, it can get pretty lonely. Teens especially crave this connection, often joining groups they wouldn't usually hang out with to feel accepted. Social media and peer pressure only make it more challenging.

The need to fit in can push us to change "who we are" just to gain acceptance. But if you're losing yourself in the process, it's time to rethink things. Adapting to what everyone else is doing and thinking is called conformity; sometimes, it can be unhealthy.

Feeling pressured to fit in and lacking a sense of belonging can lead to adverse outcomes like depression, withdrawal, anxiety, destructive behavior, substance abuse, and anger. It's a slippery slope that starts easy but gets more brutal. Research shows that 29% of students feel they don't belong at their schools (Allen, 2020).

It's essential to focus on being yourself and finding groups where you can be welcomed for who you are. As Judy Garland said, "Always be a first-rate version of yourself instead of a second-rate version of someone else." For instance, if you love art, join an art club, even if your current friends aren't into it. If you enjoy reading, find a book club.

Understanding the importance of belonging sets the foundation for building positive relationships that reflect your authentic self. Next, we'll explore core principles to guide you in developing and maintaining these connections.

Core Relationship Principles

Building positive relationships is crucial, especially at your age. As you continue to figure out who you are and prepare for your future, developing these relationship skills will significantly help you. Here are some relationship principles inspired by Dale Carnegie's book *How to Win Friends and Influence People* (2013).

- **Honesty and trust:** Always be truthful in your interactions. Honesty builds trust, which is the foundation of any strong relationship. For example, if you can't make it to a friend's event, be honest about why instead of making up an excuse.
- **Admitting mistakes:** Own up to your errors. It shows maturity, honesty, and that you value the relationship.
- **Avoid criticism and complaints:** Value others as they are. Ditch unproductive criticism, complaints, and judging. Remember, those who gossip to you will likely gossip about you. Try to understand their perspective instead of complaining about a friend's habit.
- **Empathy:** Try to see things from the other person's point of view. If a friend is stressed about an exam, remember how you felt in a similar situation.
- **Appreciate others sincerely:** Show genuine appreciation. Build people up with authentic, honest compliments. Notice and compliment others' talents, efforts, and strengths. A sincere "thank you" can make a big difference.
- **Focus on others' interests:** Show interest and enthusiasm in others' lives and passions, even if it's not your thing. Ask respectful questions and really listen to their answers.
- **Listen actively:** Pay attention when others speak. When a friend shares a story or a problem, put away your phone and really listen.
- **Friendly demeanor:** A genuine smile goes a long way. Greet people warmly, even those you don't know well.
- **Use names mindfully:** Using someone's name makes them feel valued. Try to remember and use the names of new classmates or coworkers. How do you feel when someone keeps forgetting your name? Awkward, right?

Ultimately, the core relationship principles can be summarized in two:

- **The Golden Rule:** "Treat others as you would like to be treated." This timeless principle is at the heart of all positive relationships. Before you act or speak, consider how you would feel if someone did or said the same to you.
- **Make others feel valued:** Aim to make others feel appreciated, respected, and understood in every interaction. Remember Maya Angelou's words: "I've learned that people will forget what you said, people will forget what you did, but people will never forget how you made them feel." Always prioritize making people feel valued!

These principles can help you build solid bonds with friends, family, teachers, coworkers, mentors, and anyone you meet. Building good relationships takes effort, but the rewards are worth it. As you practice these skills, you'll notice your connections flourishing and your social circle becoming a source of support, growth, and joy.

Let's explore how to apply these principles to different relationships.

The Role of Friends

> *Friendship is born at that moment when one person says to another, 'What! You too? I thought I was the only one!*
>
> C. S. Lewis

Think about how you met your best friends. Was it over a shared joke, a video game, or maybe during detention at the principal's office? Something clicked, and now you're inseparable.

Friends play a huge role as you discover who you are and where you're headed. They're likely high on your list of what's most important in your life. You might have a few close friends or be part of a big group. Some people are easy to hang out with, while others might drive you a bit crazy. Not all of them are your close, intimate friends, though.

Here's a fun list of different friend types. Can you see yourself or your friends in these?

- **The Mom/Dad:** Hovers over the group, lays down the law, and protects.
- **The Therapist:** Always there to listen and give a shoulder to cry on.
- **The Organizer:** Plans hangouts and keeps everyone connected.
- **The Joker:** Life of the party, always good for a laugh.
- **The Overachiever:** Positive, hardworking, always striving for their best.
- **The Chill One:** Relaxed, down-to-earth, nothing seems to upset them.
- **The Trendsetter:** Ahead of the curve in style and interests.
- **The Hot Head:** Strong-willed, opinionated, and quick to fight.
- **The Pessimist:** Alarmed by the latest news, always trying to keep everyone safe.
- **The Mess:** Always losing things and never having anything together.

The funny thing is that as much as we tend to see friends as one or another of the stereotypes mentioned above, most of us are a blend of these "personas." We can be chill or emotional, the joker or the overachiever, organized and messy in different aspects of life. It's essential to see that there is more to a person than they seem... and that it's worth getting to know people in all their facets.

Qualities of Good Friendships

Not all friendships have to be super-close. You may have best friends, acquaintances, and people you enjoy spending time with occasionally. As you grow, you become more discerning about who you open up to. These people become your good friends, and you may notice that your relationships with them are built on the following qualities:

- **Shared interests and values:** You have similar views on important issues.
- **Trustworthiness and honesty:** You can tell them your secrets without worrying they'll spill them on others.

- **Loyalty and reliability:** They stick by you through thick and thin and vice versa.
- **Mutual respect:** They respect your choices, even if they differ from theirs.
- **Empathy and support:** When you are stressed, they listen and offer emotional support and encouragement.
- **Acceptance:** You accept each other's quirks without harsh judgment.
- **Open communication:** You can have honest conversations, even about difficult topics.
- **Ability to resolve conflicts:** When you disagree, you can talk it out and find a solution together.
- **Positivity and fun:** You have a great time together, whether doing something exciting or just hanging out.

Building friendships based on these qualities can lead to meaningful, fulfilling, and long-lasting relationships that enrich your life throughout your teenage years and beyond.

The Impact of Friendships

Having friends is about more than just having people to spend time with. Studies show that close friendships help teens (Abrams, 2023):

- Adapt to stress better.
- Have higher self-esteem.
- Improve mental health.
- Perform better academically.

A robust support system acts as a buffer against life's challenges.

Build and Maintain Healthy Friendships

If you're finding it a bit hard to make close friends or expand your friendship group, remember that quality matters more than quantity. Here are some practical ways to make new friends and strengthen existing friendships:

- **Choose friends wisely:** Surround yourself with positive influences. For instance,

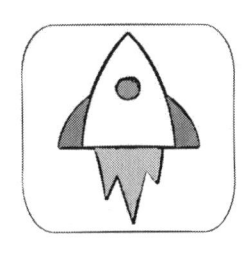

befriend classmates who take their studies seriously if you want to do well in school.
- **Nurture the friendship:**

    o *Show appreciation:* Tell your friends you value their support during a tough time.
    o *Support each other:* Cheer them on at their sports game or art show.
    o *Stay in touch:* A quick check-up text can keep your bond strong.
    o *Make lasting memories:* Plan fun activities together, like a movie night or a hike.

- **Communicate effectively:** Learn to express yourself clearly and listen actively. If there's a misunderstanding, address it calmly and openly.
- **Be yourself:** Don't pretend to like something just to fit in. Your true interests will attract friends who appreciate the real you.
- **Make an effort:** Join clubs or sports teams that interest you. It's a great way to meet like-minded people.
- **Accept others:** Be open-minded about differences. You might learn something new from a friend with a different background or perspective.

Building and maintaining friendships takes time and effort, but it's worth it. These relationships can provide joy, support, and personal growth. As you practice these skills, you'll be surrounded by friends who truly get you and have your back.

Home Is Where the Heart Is

Imagine an elastic band. Stretch it out and hold it for a while. Your arms get tired from the tension, right? That's much like your relationship with your parents during your teen years. You need them, but you also crave independence. It's a push-pull that can be exhausting for everyone involved.

As you grow up, your relationship with your parents changes dramatically. They go from being your heroes to sometimes feeling a bit overbearing. But have you considered how your parents are also trying to adapt to your changes? When you were little, they were your caregivers. Then, they became your teachers and guides. Now, they're more like coaches or advisers. They're learning on the job, just like you!

Take a moment to reflect: What would you give it if you had to rate your relationship with your mother or father out of ten (with ten being perfect)? How about with your siblings?

Benefits of Strong Family Bonds

Maintaining solid relationships with your family is crucial for your growth. Here's why:

- **Positive influence:** Your parents and siblings are potentially your biggest cheerleaders. They usually want the best for you even when it doesn't feel like it.
- **Emotional support:** Your family can support you during tough times, offering a safe space to express your emotions.
- **A sense of belonging:** Strong family bonds give you a sense of security and self-confidence. It grounds you!
- **Open communication:** Healthy family relationships teach you how to communicate and resolve conflicts effectively.

As the saying goes, *"Family is where life begins, and love never ends."*

Build and Maintain Healthy Family Ties

Here are some tips to keep your family relationships solid:

- **Open up:** Don't isolate yourself. Instead of heading straight to your room after school, try chatting with your family about your day. A funny moment at school?
- **Engage:** Keep communication lines open. Ask a parent or sibling for input if you're working on a school project. Their perspective might surprise you!
- **Make memories now:** Time flies! Before you know it, you'll be adulting, and family hangouts will be rare. Grab every chance to chill with the fam – game nights, movie marathons, or goofing around. These moments? They're your future nostalgia gold. Cherish them!
- **Respect:** Avoid badmouthing your family to your friends. If your friends complain about their families, try changing the subject or

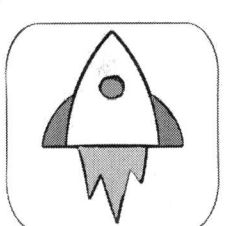

sharing something positive about yours. Remember, everyone's family dynamic is different.
- **Show appreciation:** Recognize your family members' efforts. Thank your parents for their support, even for small things like making your favorite meal. Tell your siblings you appreciate them – maybe offer to help with their chores or treat them to ice cream.

The Extended Squad

Don't forget about your backup crew —grandparents, aunts, uncles, and cousins! These folks are like your secret weapon of support and fun.

- **Grandparents** are walking history books with the best stories and wisdom (and often the best snacks). Ask them about their childhood and see their eyes light up!
- **Aunts and uncles** can be your cool adult friends who give fantastic advice. They might serve as an additional source of guidance than your parents on things like career choices or relationships.
- **Cousins?** Instant party squad! Plan regular hangouts or start a group chat to stay connected.

Nurture these bonds, and you'll have a whole network of people cheering you on. They can offer different perspectives, share family traditions, and be there when you need an extra boost. Plus, family reunions become way more fun when you actually know and like your extended family. Sharing inside stories about the "crazy uncle"? Priceless!

Remember, your family is your support system. Putting in the effort to keep these relationships strong can make your home life much happier. As Jem from *To Kill a Mockingbird* said, "You can choose your friends, but you sho' can't choose your family, an' they're still kin to you no matter whether you acknowledge 'em or not."

So, reach out, stay connected, and watch your family support system grow. It's an investment in relationships that can last a lifetime!

Role Models and Trusted Advisers

> *Mentoring is a brain to pick, an ear to listen, and a push in the right direction.*
>
> John C. Crosby

While your family can be a robust support system, sometimes you need guidance outside your immediate circle. This is where role models and mentors come in, offering valuable insights and support based on their experiences.

Who You Want to Be Like

Role models can be anyone you admire for their character and achievements. They might be:

- A teacher who inspires you to pursue a subject you love.
- An athlete who demonstrates incredible perseverance.
- A historical figure who stood up for their beliefs.

These role models influence your attitudes, help you make healthy choices, and boost your self-esteem—even after they are gone. Family members can also be role models!

Reflect on these questions:

- Who do you look up to or want to be like?
- What specific qualities do you admire in them?
- Can you identify celebrities or influencers who might not be good role models? Why?

Who You Want to Listen To

Mentors and advisers may differ from role models. They offer personalized wisdom and guidance based on their experiences. A good mentor can boost confidence, provide insights, and support decisions. Think about:

- The coach who gives you tips on improving your skills.

- Your supportive family friend who helps you explore career options.
- Your older cousin who's always there to listen when you're in trouble.

Finding a Good Mentor

Here's how you can find a mentor who's right for you:

- **Define your goals:** Know what you want to achieve. If you're struggling with writing, seek a teacher known for their writing skills.
- **Choose someone who knows you:** Look for someone familiar with your background and environment. An older sibling or aunt might understand your family dynamics better than an outsider.
- **Ask for what you want:** Be clear about why you need a mentor and how they can help. For example, ask a family friend if they can meet regularly to discuss your career path.
- **Contribute to the relationship:** Remember, it's a two-way street. Share your thoughts during discussions, offer to help with tasks they might struggle with (like technology), or simply share stories to brighten their day.

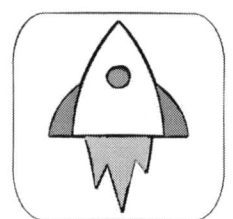

Can you develop a list of two to five people you could reach out to for support or mentorship?

The Power of Networking

Building connections with like-minded individuals, mentors, and even industry leaders can open doors you never imagined. While you might think networking is just for adults, starting early can give you a huge advantage.

Why Networking Matters for Teens

- It can help you discover potential career paths.
- You might find opportunities for internships or part-time jobs.
- It teaches you valuable communication skills.
- You can learn about different industries and roles firsthand.

Best Practices for Networking

- **Start early:** Begin building your network before you need it. Think about people you've worked for, even if it was just babysitting or mowing lawns. Reach out and ask for recommendations.
- **Leverage existing connections:** Start with people you already know. Ask a family friend working in a field you're interested in for advice. Suggest meeting for a coffee or a quick video chat.
- **Attend events:** Go to relevant events online or in person. Participate in virtual career fairs or local industry meet-ups that welcome students.
- **Get involved:** Join clubs and organizations related to your interests. You'll meet like-minded people and potential mentors.
- **Use social media wisely:** Even if you've just started working or have a part-time or freelance job, create a professional profile on LinkedIn or use other platforms to follow and engage with people in fields you're interested in.
- **Prepare and practice:** Prepare a short introduction about yourself, your interests, and your goals, also called an "elevator pitch." Practice it so you feel confident when meeting new people.
- **Follow-up:** After meeting someone, send a thank-you message. To help them remember you, mention something specific you discussed.
- **Offer value:** Look for ways to assist your connections. Share interesting articles, introduce them to others who might be helpful, or offer your skills (like managing social media).
- **Be genuine:** Build authentic relationships. Approach networking with a real interest in learning from others.

Networking is a long-term investment in your personal and professional growth. By consistently putting in effort, being authentic, and offering value to others, you'll gradually build a solid network to support you throughout your journey.

Can you develop a list of five to ten people or organizations you can contact to build your network?

Building Your Inner Circle

Imagine dropping a stone into a calm lake. The ripples closest to the point of impact are strong and defined, while those further out become fainter. Your relationships work similarly – some people are close to your core, creating powerful impacts, while others are more distant influences.

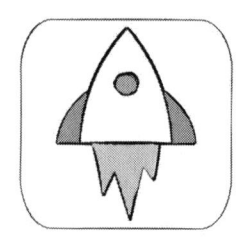

British anthropologist Robin Dunbar suggests humans can only maintain about 150 meaningful connections. But not all of these connections are equal. Dunbar's research indicates different layers of relationships:

- 5 loved ones
- 15 good friends
- 50 friends
- 150 meaningful contacts
- 500 acquaintances
- 1500 people you can recognize

In the age of social media, these lines can get blurred, and "friend" counts can easily exceed these numbers. It's crucial to distinguish between your true inner circle and your broader network. Your inner circle should be tight, meaningful, and supportive of your growth and well-being.

Why Your Inner Circle Matters

Your inner circle is pivotal in shaping who you become. These are the people who:

- Influence your decisions and behaviors.
- Provide emotional support during challenging times.
- Celebrate your successes and help you learn from failures.
- Shape your perspectives and values.

For example, if your inner circle includes academically motivated friends, you're more likely to prioritize your studies. If your circle includes people who engage in risky behaviors, you might be more tempted to do the same. It might be time to reshuffle.

Identifying Your Inner Circle

Try this exercise to identify your current inner circle:

- Write down 4 to 5 names of your best friends.
- List 4 to 5 family members you're closest to.
- Note 2 to 3 mentors or advisers who guide you.

Now, reflect on these questions:

- Do these people genuinely support you and have your best interests at heart?
- Why do you spend time with them?
- Do they teach you new things or help you improve?
- How do you feel after spending time with them?

Qualities to Look for in Your Inner Circle

As you evaluate and potentially reshape your inner circle, look for these qualities:

- **Giving:** They are generous with their time and support.
- **Authentic:** They tell you the truth, even when it's not what you want to hear.
- **Accountable:** They check in on you and ensure you stay on track with your goals.
- **Non-judgmental:** They accept you for who you are.
- **Trustworthy:** They keep your confidence.

Your inner circle isn't limited to just friends. It can include family members, mentors, or even teachers who genuinely support and uplift you.

Managing Your Inner Circle

As you grow and change, your inner circle may shift. This is normal and healthy. Here are some tips for managing your inner circle:

- **Regular evaluation:** Periodically assess who's in your inner circle and why.
- **Quality over quantity:** Focus on deepening a few key relationships rather than maintaining many superficial ones.
- **Be open to change:** As your interests and goals evolve, be open to new connections that align with your growth.
- **Boundaries:** Learn to set healthy boundaries, even with those in your inner circle.
- **Reciprocity:** Ensure you give as much as you receive in these relationships.

These core relationships will provide the support, challenge, and inspiration you need to navigate your teen years and beyond.

Shielding Your Inner Circle

You've just explored the rewarding world of relationships. Here's a quick recap of key takeaways:

- Your social circle profoundly shapes who you become — choose wisely.
- Healthy relationships are built on trust, respect, and open communication.
- Family bonds, friendships, and mentorships are crucial to your personal growth.
- Building a robust inner circle takes time and effort, but it's one of the most valuable investments you can make.

Remember, the goal isn't to be popular or to have hundreds of superficial connections. It's about cultivating meaningful relationships that enrich your life and help you become the best version of yourself.

Next, we'll explore a special connection often taking center stage in teen life. Get ready to dive into matters of the heart!

SEVEN

Matters of The Heart

> *Love is friendship that has caught fire.*
>
> Ann Landers

Love at first sight. An instant connection. Stars aligned. It sounds like a movie or a cheesy romance book. As you navigate your teen years, you might find yourself experiencing intense emotions and attractions. Suddenly, people around you look different. An irritating classmate unexpectedly becomes the highlight of your day or a friend you never thought of romantically becomes incredibly attractive.

Your heart races when they pass, and you start daydreaming about shared moments. Welcome to the exciting, confusing, and sometimes overwhelming world of crushes, first loves, and romantic relationships!

While these feelings can be exhilarating, it's vital to approach romance with both enthusiasm and caution. This chapter will explore the difference between infatuation and love, recognize healthy and unhealthy partners, and discover self-love's crucial role in forming meaningful bonds.

Keep in mind the valuable insights we've already discussed about friendships, family, building an inner circle, and self-awareness. These form the foundation upon which healthy romantic relationships are built.

So, are you ready to untangle the mysteries of the heart? Let's begin!

Love vs. Infatuation

Try to guess which statements describe love and which describe infatuation:

1. Very emotional
2. Focused more on character than looks
3. Looking for one's happiness through the other person
4. Feelings arise very suddenly
5. Is willing to wait
6. Is not jealous
7. Temporary
8. Communication is more important than touch
9. Always worried about what they think of you
10. Accept their imperfections

Answers:

1. Infatuation: It's based on intense, often fleeting emotions.
2. Love: It values the whole person, not just physical appearance.
3. Infatuation: It seeks fulfillment solely from the other person.
4. Infatuation: It develops quickly without deep knowledge of the person.
5. Love: It understands that bonds take time to develop.
6. Love: It's based on trust and security.
7. Infatuation: It often fades as quickly as it appears.
8. Love: It prioritizes understanding and connection.
9. Infatuation: It's often insecure and seeks constant validation.
10. Love: It acknowledges that everyone has flaws.

How did you do? Understanding love and infatuation can help you navigate your feelings and relationships more effectively.

According to therapist Jack Hazan, healthy romantic bonds require three things—not one or two, all three!

- **Trust:** This means being honest with each other, not keeping secrets, maintaining a sense of security, and knowing they won't physically, emotionally, or mentally hurt you.
- **Communication:** Talking openly about feelings, needs, and concerns. This includes active listening and having difficult

conversations when necessary. You connect and understand each other well.
- **Respect:** You value each other for who you are. Respect boundaries, opinions, beliefs, and choices.

If any of these three ingredients is absent in your partnership, it's most likely infatuation.

Self-Love: The Foundation of Healthy Relationships

Before diving into a love relationship head first, prioritize cultivating a strong sense of self-love and embrace solitude. Learning to be comfortable alone is crucial for personal growth and healthy relationships.

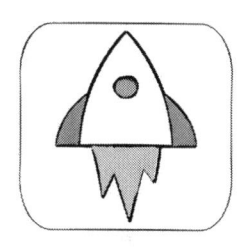

Here are ways to boost self-love and appreciate solitude:

- Practice self-compassion and positive self-talk
- Set personal boundaries
- Pursue interests and hobbies
- Celebrate achievements
- Surround yourself with positive influences
- Accept mistakes as growth opportunities
- Express gratitude
- Take care of physical and mental health
- Seek professional help if needed

Embrace alone time as an opportunity for self-discovery and growth. Use it to:

- Reflect on personal values and goals
- Develop independence and self-reliance
- Cultivate creativity and pursue passions
- Practice mindfulness and self-care

Who Do We Spend Our Lifetime With
(avg. time per day)

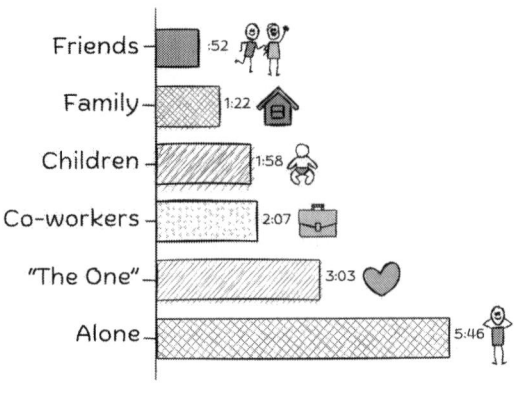

- Friends: :52
- Family: 1:22
- Children: 1:58
- Co-workers: 2:07
- "The One": 3:03
- Alone: 5:46

Source: ourworldindata.org

The most significant human relationship you'll ever have is with yourself. Our World in Data study reveals that Americans spend most of their time alone.

When you're comfortable alone and value yourself, you're better equipped to form healthy connections with others, including friends, family, and romantic partners. You will be equipped to pursue healthy connections and set appropriate boundaries.

Don't enter relationships out of fear of being alone. Instead, approach them from a place of self-assurance and completeness. This mindset allows you to form more authentic and balanced connections.

Red Flags

While cultivating self-love and comfort with solitude provides a strong foundation, it's equally important to recognize the dynamics of our relationships with others. We must know healthy and unhealthy patterns as we interact with friends, family, coworkers, and romantic partners. Let's explore some red flags that signal potentially toxic relationships, helping us maintain the self-respect and boundaries we've worked to establish.

- **Emotional red flags:**

  - Constant criticism or belittling
  - Emotional manipulation (guilt-tripping, silent treatment)
  - Jealousy or possessiveness
  - Resentment
  - Feeling consistently stressed or anxious
  - Emotional exhaustion

- **Behavioral red flags:**

  - Controlling behaviors (dictating who you see or what you do)
  - Ignoring boundaries
  - Intentionally avoiding each other
  - Encouraging risky or unethical behaviors
  - Any form of aggression: physical, emotional, or mental

- **Communication red flags:**

  - Lack of trust and honesty
  - Constant unresolved conflicts
  - Inability to have open, respectful discussions
  - One-sided communication

- **Respect red flags:**

  - Feeling unappreciated
  - Disregard for privacy or personal space
  - Unhealthy competition or resentment
  - Lack of mutual respect for each other's opinions, beliefs, or choices

If you notice any of these symptoms, taking them seriously is essential. Remember, you deserve to feel valued, loved, cared for, respected, and supported. Otherwise, it's okay to move on.

Coping with Toxic Relationships:

When dealing with these issues, time is of the essence. Like a cavity that worsens if left untreated, toxic dynamics can cause lasting damage if ignored. It's crucial to address these issues promptly and effectively. Here are some strategies to help you navigate and heal from toxic relationships:

- Acknowledge the problem
- Find the root cause
- Communicate effectively
- Set clear boundaries
- Confide in someone you trust
- Take a break if needed
- End the relationship if necessary
- Practice self-compassion
- Reflect and learn from the experience
- Surround yourself with positivity

Seeking Help

If you are in an unhealthy situation affecting your well-being, seek help! Here are some options:

- Confide in a trusted adult
- Connect with helplines or support groups
- Open up to a close friend
- Consult a professional if needed
- Alert authorities if you feel in danger

Reaching out for support is a sign of strength.

Nurturing Your Heart

As you navigate the exciting and sometimes confusing world of romantic relationships, keep these critical points in mind:

- Understanding the difference between love and infatuation can help you navigate emotions more effectively.
- True love develops over time.
- Healthy relationships are built on trust, communication, and mutual respect.
- Self-love and personal growth are the foundations for healthy romantic connections.
- Recognizing red flags early can protect you from potentially harmful relationships. Trust your instincts and seek help if needed.
- Taking things slowly is okay.

Your worth isn't determined by your relationship status. Whether single, dating, or committed, staying true to yourself and your values is essential.

In the next chapter, we'll explore strategies for navigating the storms that can arise in all types of relationships, not only romantic ones. We are talking about peer pressure, conflicts, drama…

EIGHT

Navigating Relationship Storms

> *You can't just give up on someone just because the situation is not ideal. Great relationships aren't great because they have no problems. They're great because both people care about the other person to find a way to make it work.*
>
> Anonymous

Navigating relationships is like sailing through unpredictable waters. Break-ups, arguments, drama, betrayals, and rivalries are all part of the journey. Our emotions are at the heart of these storms – powerful forces that can guide us to safe harbors or lead us astray.

As you grow and change, so do your relationships. Your circle of trust evolves, with people moving closer or drifting apart. This constant flux is natural but can be challenging to manage. The key to weathering these storms lies in understanding and regulating your emotions and empathizing with others.

This chapter will explore navigating relationship dynamics, handling peer pressure, resolving conflicts, and practicing forgiveness. We'll also delve into the crucial role of emotional intelligence in maintaining healthy connections. By mastering these skills, you'll be better equipped to steer through the choppy waters of relationships with confidence and resilience.

Relationship Dynamics

Here are some reasons relationship dynamics are fluid. It's important to acknowledge them, embrace them, and move on, if necessary:

- **Shifting priorities and interests:** As you grow and discover new passions, you might find that you and your friends don't always see eye to eye. It's normal for your interests to evolve, which can sometimes cause friction or create distance in your friendships.
- **Peer pressure:** Wanting to fit in and be accepted by your peers can sometimes push you to do uncomfortable things. This pressure can strain friendships, especially if it means compromising your values.
- **Cliques and social hierarchies:** Friend groups sometimes feel exclusive, creating a sense of competition and pressure to conform. This can lead to feelings of exclusion and tension.
- **Changing schools or moving:** Switching schools or moving to a new area can shake your social life. Becoming accustomed to new environments and making new friends can be challenging and might affect your existing friendships.
- **Diverging paths:** As you get closer to finishing high school, your future plans might differ from those of your friends. Whether it's college, work, or other aspirations, these diverging paths can lead to growing apart.
- **Romantic relationships:** Introducing a romantic relationship into the mix can sometimes shift the balance of your friendships. Finding time for your partner and your friends can be tricky and may cause tension.
- **Lack of communication and conflict resolution skills:** Effective communication is key but not always easy. Misunderstandings and unresolved conflicts can cause rifts in friendships if you don't have the skills to talk things out.
- **Jealousy and insecurity:** Sometimes, it's normal to feel jealous or insecure, especially regarding things like romantic interests or academic achievements. However, these feelings can lead to unhealthy competition and tension among friends.
- **Bullying and peer victimization:** Whether in person or online, bullying can severely impact your friendships and well-being, leading to isolation and low self-esteem.

Dealing with these challenges through open communication, empathy, respect, and guidance can help you develop healthy coping strategies and maintain meaningful friendships during this transitional phase.

Peer Pressure

Ever felt like your friends are pushing you to do something you're not totally cool with? That's peer pressure tugging your inner cords! Dealing with pressure from friends and those around you can be challenging, and sometimes, it's hard to resist.

Let's learn a few strategies to assist you in handling peer pressure and staying true to yourself:

- **Just say nope:** It takes guts, but "No" is a complete sentence that sends a clear message.

  - A straight-up "Nah, I'm good" works wonders.
  - Flip the script: "Hey, why don't we do this instead?"
  - Turn it back on them: "Come on, if you were really my friend, you wouldn't push me."

- **Dodge and weave:**

  - Pretend you didn't hear and change the subject.
  - Pull the parent card: "My folks would kill me if I did that."
  - If things get weird, it's okay to bail.

- **Call in the cavalry:**

  - Get your squad to back you up: "Guys, help me out here."
  - When in doubt, talk to an adult you trust.

- **Think it through:**

  - Are your friends really looking out for you?
  - It may be time to find some new buddies who get you.

Not all peer pressure is bad news. Sometimes, your friends push you to try new stuff or up your awesome game. The trick is figuring out what feels and is right for you.

Standing up for yourself might initially feel awkward. Real friends will respect your choices, no matter what. So go ahead, be yourself – it's your superpower!

Social Media Pressure

Numerous studies have shown that social media platforms can be highly addictive and are often linked to anxiety, depression, and even physical ailments. One of the reasons people keep coming back is the unpredictable nature of the outcome – similar to a slot machine, where the possibility of a reward (like a "like" or comment) keeps you coming back for more (Mass General Brigham McLean, n.d.).

Social media has its upsides. It enables you to keep in contact with distant friends and family and can be entertaining and informative. However, it also has significant downsides:

- **Excessive comparison:** Constantly measuring your life against others' curated posts can lead to feelings of inadequacy or envy.
- **Cyberbullying and drama:** Online bullying, exclusion, or gossip can create a toxic environment.
- **Reduced face-to-face interaction:** Overreliance on online communication can weaken real-world social skills and connections.
- **Fear of missing out (FOMO):** Seeing posts about events you weren't invited to can trigger feelings of exclusion.
- **Negative self-image:** Exposure to idealized posts can impact your body image and self-esteem.
- **Distraction:** Excessive use can interfere with real-world activities and in-person interactions.

If you notice these signs, it might be time to reassess your social media habits.

Dealing with Social Media Challenges

Here are some strategies to manage these challenges:

- **Open communication:** Discuss with friends how social media impacts your relationships and set boundaries together.
- **Prioritize in-person interactions:** Make an effort to spend quality time with friends offline.
- **Reality check:** Remember that social media presents filtered versions of people's lives, not the whole picture.
- **Be a positive influence:** Lead by example online by being respectful, kind, and supportive.
- **Limit FOMO:** Focus on being present in your own life rather than constantly checking what others are doing.
- **Reduce or eliminate use:** Consider taking breaks from social media or deleting apps altogether to reduce their impact on your mental health.
- **Seek help:** If social media is causing significant stress or anxiety, don't hesitate to talk to a trusted adult or mental health professional.

By being aware of these challenges and implementing these strategies, you can maintain a healthier relationship with social media and protect your mental well-being.

Conflict Resolution

Conflict is a part of life! It's what happens when you put a group of people together in a class, team, or family.

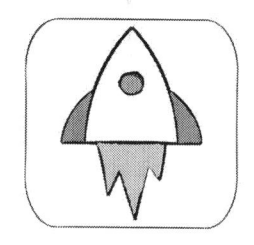

Picture this: You're psyched about your group project idea, but your teammate shoots it down. Cue the awkward silence and rising tension. Welcome to the world of conflict!

If not dealt with, they can strain relationships, cause anxiety, and lead to severe problems.

Conflict isn't always destructive. If handled well, it can be healthy and strengthen relationships. An old saying goes, "iron sharpens iron," meaning that challenges can make us better and stronger.

Steps to Resolve Conflicts

So, how do you turn a potential blow-up into a breakthrough? Here are a few steps to help you manage those tense moments:

1. **Don't hide:** Avoid sticking your head in the sand and hoping the conflict will blow over. Tackle it head-on before it snowballs.
2. **Listen up:** Before jumping in with your side, hear the other person out. And we're talking full attention (body and all) —no scrolling on your phone, pointing fingers, crossing arms, or planning your comeback.
3. **Keep it cool:** When emotions are running hot, chill your voice. Yelling? That's just going to make things worse.
4. **Focus on the problem, not the person:** Instead of "You always mess things up!" try "I'm worried about how this affects our project."
5. **Win-win it:** If you both try to "win," nobody does. Be ready to meet in the middle.
6. **Sorry seems to be the hardest word:** Apologies can be tough to deliver, but they're game-changers. Practice in the mirror if you need to! A sincere apology can diffuse an entire argument.
7. **Call for backup:** Ask a trusted source to play referee if you're stuck.

When things get heated, remember the PEN method:

- **Pause:** Take a breather. Count to ten. Whatever stops you from saying something that you'll regret later.
- **Empathy:** Try to see where they're coming from. Everyone's fighting their own battles, you know?
- **Needs:** Share what you need and hope for. Look for a solution that works for both of you.

But what if your best efforts fall flat? Don't sweat it. Sometimes, you might need to:

- **Take a time-out:** A little space can do wonders.
- **Seek outside help:** A trusted adult might offer a fresh perspective.
- **Agree to disagree:** It's okay if you can't see eye-to-eye on everything.

Conflict resolution is a skill. The more you practice, the better you'll get. You might be surprised at how quickly you can turn a potential fight into a chance to understand each other better. Who knows? That person you're butting heads with today might become your closest ally tomorrow!

Forgiveness and Moving Forward

Ever been hurt by a friend and thought, "No way I'm forgiving them!"? It's normal to feel that way, and it can be hard to forgive them. You may fear that doing so will open yourself up to further hurt. But here's the plot twist: forgiveness isn't about letting someone off the hook —it's about freeing yourself!

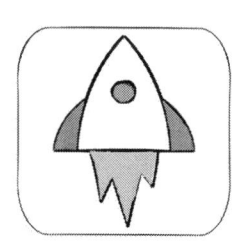

Forgiveness doesn't mean forgetting or admitting what happened was okay. You can even forgive without getting an apology! Think about all the emotions and time spent discussing the issue. Is it really worth the drama? By not forgiving, you let that person live "rent-free" in your head!

Why bother forgiving? Forgiveness can reduce stress, improve mental health, and strengthen relationships. It can also boost your self-esteem and overall life satisfaction. On the other hand, holding onto anger, resentment, and hate can lead to depression and a cycle of negativity that affects all aspects of life.

Practicing Forgiveness

- **Forgiving others:** It's an inside job. You can forgive even if the other person doesn't apologize. For example, if a friend betrays your trust, you might forgive them internally for your peace of mind, regardless of their actions.
- **Accepting forgiveness:** Accepting forgiveness is as essential as forgiving. It's tricky but crucial for moving forward. For instance, if that same friend who betrayed you reaches out to ask for forgiveness, accept it and move on!
- **Self-forgiveness:** Often, the most complicated person to forgive is ourselves. We hold on to guilt and self-loathing for things we did or said. Cut yourself some slack! For example, if you made a mistake that cost your team a game, learn from it, but don't let it define you. Forgive yourself and focus on improving.

EQ: Your Relationship Compass

At the core of every relationship storm lies a whirlwind of emotions. Emotional intelligence (EQ) is your compass to help you navigate choppy waters. It's the ability to recognize, understand, and manage emotions—both yours and others.

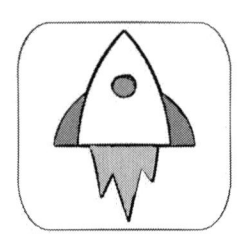

When conflicts arise or peer pressure mounts, your EQ can mean the difference between a smooth resolution and a relationship shipwreck. By honing this skill, you'll be better equipped to handle the ups and downs of friendships, family dynamics, and romantic partnerships.

The four pillars of emotional intelligence:

1. **Self-awareness:** Recognizing your thoughts and emotions and understanding how they impact your behavior. For example, realizing that you tend to withdraw when feeling overwhelmed.
2. **Self-management:** Regulating your emotions, especially in challenging situations. Like taking a deep breath and counting to ten when you're angry instead of lashing out.
3. **Social awareness:** Picking up on others' emotions and understanding their perspectives. This might involve noticing that your friend seems down because of a recent break-up.
4. **Relationship management:** Using empathy and emotional understanding to interact positively with others and resolve conflicts. For instance, consider your brother's feelings when you're arguing about whose turn it is to do the dishes and knowing he has a big test tomorrow.

Identifying Emotions

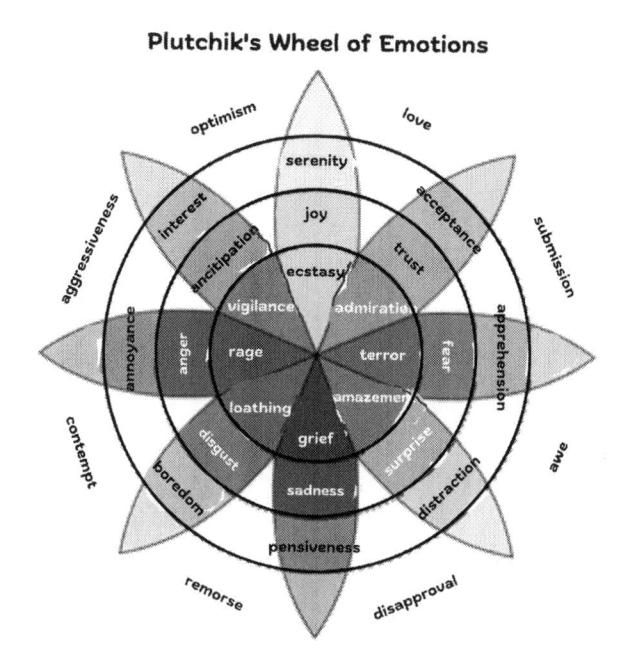

Plutchik's Wheel of Emotions

Emotions are complex and nuanced. While we often talk about basic feelings like happiness, sadness, and anger, we experience a spectrum of emotions daily. Plutchik's Wheel of Emotions is a helpful tool for understanding this spectrum.

This wheel showcases eight basic emotions: joy, trust, fear, surprise, sadness, disgust, anger, and anticipation. It also shows how these emotions can intensify or combine to create more complex feelings. For example, anger in its mildest form is annoyance, but at its most intense, it becomes rage.

Try using this wheel in your daily life:

- Pause periodically to check in with yourself.
- Identify which emotion on the wheel best matches how you feel.
- Note the intensity of the emotion.
- Consider what triggered this feeling.

By practicing this regularly, you'll become more attuned to your emotional state, improving your **self-awareness** and the ability to recognize emotions in others **(social awareness)**.

Regulating and Managing Emotions

Emotional regulation can be particularly challenging for teens. Your brain, especially the prefrontal cortex responsible for reasoned judgments, is still developing until age 25. But don't worry—awareness of this fact is the first step to better emotional self-management.

When you find yourself in an emotionally charged situation, try this four-step approach:

1. **Stop:** Pause and take a breath. Count to ten or close your eyes until you feel more in control. This takes practice, but it gets easier with time.
2. **Admit:** Don't ignore or push down your feelings. Accept them as part of you. Even negative emotions like anger can be helpful signals that something needs to change.
3. **Ask:** Reflect on your reaction. Was it justified? What could you have done differently? What should you do next? Is an apology needed?
4. **Accept:** Take responsibility for your actions. If you responded harshly, apologize sincerely. People will respect your maturity, and it's a healthy step forward.

Empathy: Building Bridges

Empathy is the cornerstone of emotional intelligence and effective relationship management. It's not about feeling sorry for someone but genuinely understanding their perspective and emotions.

Imagine you're crossing a bridge into someone else's world. What do you see from their vantage point? How might they be feeling? What might be influencing their actions or reactions?

Practicing empathy involves:

- Active listening without judgment
- Recognizing and validating others' emotions
- Considering how your actions might impact others

For example, suppose your friend is upset about not making the team. Instead of immediately trying to cheer them up or offer solutions, you might say, "That must be really disappointing. Do you want to talk about how you're feeling?"

Cultivating empathy will make you a more compassionate friend, partner, and leader. You'll also be better equipped to navigate conflicts, strengthen your bonds, and weather any relationship storm.

Connection Corner

Strengthen your relationships and emotional intelligence with these activities:

Journal Prompts

- List five things you love about yourself.
- Reflect on your ideal romantic partner. What qualities are most important to you? How do these align with your own values and goals?
- Describe your favorite family tradition or a cherished memory with your family.
- Write about a time when a friend went above and beyond for you or when you shared an unforgettable experience together.
- Describe your ideal mentor. What qualities do they possess?
- When I get angry with someone, I...
- In a disagreement, I find it most challenging to...
- A conflict that didn't end well was... I could have...
- Describe a time you felt peer pressure. How did you handle it? What would you do differently now?
- Think about a challenging moment with a family member. How could you apply the conflict resolution steps we discussed to improve the situation?
- Write your "elevator pitch" for networking situations.

Activity

- Create a visual map of your relationships, including friends, family, mentors, "the one," and acquaintances. For each person, write:

    - What have I received from this person?

- What have I given to this person?
- What troubles and difficulties have I caused this person?

• Use Plutchik's Wheel of Emotions to identify and track your emotions for a week.

Unlock Your Connection Corner Toolkit

Scan the QR code below for extra tips and tools to effectively connect with people. Keep checking back for fresh content!

The Takeaway

Relationships can be special and unique, but they can also be complicated and stormy. Remember that your emotions are the wind in your sails and the rudder that steers your ship away from troubled waters. By developing emotional intelligence, you'll be better equipped to handle the complexities of relationships, from friendships to romantic partnerships.

Every storm eventually passes. With these skills in your toolkit, you'll weather the challenges and emerge stronger, with deeper, more meaningful connections.

If you're keeping track, we've covered three directions of your life as a young adult: North, East, and South. We're about to swing West into a territory at the root of many relationship dramas. Ready to discover what it is?

Part Four: West

CASH COURSE

The Financial Whiz: *This savvy individual transforms financial literacy into real-world success. They understand the power of money as a tool for freedom and impact, excelling in the art of earning, saving, and growing wealth while aligning their finances with their values.*

NINE

Making Bank

> *You say love is more important than money. But have you ever tried paying your bills with a hug?*
>
> Anonymous

In the previous chapters, we discussed the complexities of relationships and the challenges that come with them. But did you know that money can make or break even the strongest bonds? According to a study, 38% of people surveyed cited financial problems as a reason for divorce (Bieber, 2024). Moreover, nearly 73% of Americans say that money issues are a significant source of stress in their lives (White, 2024).

Warren Buffett, one of the world's most successful businesspeople and investors, has an important message for kids and teens: you don't have to wait until you are in your twenties or thirties to start earning, saving, and investing money. In fact, he recommends that parents start teaching their kids about financial literacy in preschool.

So, what exactly is financial literacy? It means understanding various financial skills and concepts—including the importance of making money and keeping most of it while planning for future needs. When financially literate, you are less vulnerable to financial fraud and trouble. You are also more able to achieve your life goals—including saving for your education, buying a home, and retiring comfortably.

What's Your Money Personality?

Before we dive into the nitty-gritty, let's start with a quick and fun exercise to evaluate your money tendencies. Answer these questions based on how you typically handle money:

Scenario 1: You just received your first paycheck. What's your first move?

A) Treat yourself to something nice you've been eyeing.
B) Save a portion and spend the rest on necessities.
C) Invest in something that will grow over time.
D) Pay off any debts you have and then decide.

Scenario 2: Your friends invite you on a spontaneous weekend trip, but it's a bit pricey. What do you do?

A) Go for it! Experiences are worth every penny, even if credit card sponsored.
B) Suggest a more affordable alternative or plan for a future trip.
C) Politely decline and save your money for something more appealing in the future.
D) Check your budget and see if you can swing it without messing up your finances.

Scenario 3: Your favorite store is having a massive sale. What's your reaction?

A) Time to shop till you drop!
B) Buy only what you need or have planned for.
C) Skip the sale and invest that money instead.
D) Avoid the temptation and stick to your budget.

Tally Your Answers:

- *Mostly As:* You love enjoying your money now, but watch out for overspending.
- *Mostly Bs:* You're a Saver! You're good at balancing fun and responsibility with your money.
- *Mostly Cs:* You're an Investor! You're always looking for ways to grow your wealth.

- *Mostly Ds:* You're a Planner! You focus on financial security and making well-thought-out decisions.

Regarding money, we'll cover seven key areas: banking, earning, spending, borrowing, saving, investing, and budgeting. Each area plays a crucial role, and it's essential to understand how they all work together.

Banking Basics: Your Money's New Home

Keeping your money in a piggy bank was fun when you were little. But in today's digital world, you can access your money in various ways—through a plastic or virtual card, phone, or even wearable tech like smartwatches. Think of banks as a place to keep your money and help you manage it wisely.

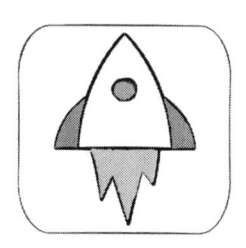

First, let's talk about the main types of bank accounts: checking and savings.

Checking Account

Your checking account is like your wallet. It's where you keep the money for everyday expenses, like grabbing lunch with friends, paying for gas, handling those never-ending subscriptions, or buying that fabulous outfit you saw online.

You can access your cash anytime with a debit card, Venmo, Zelle, or other tools linked directly to your checking account. Remember that once you swipe, the money is gone, so it's essential to keep an eye on that cash balance so you don't go into overdraft!

Overdraft is when you spend more cash than you have in your account. Of course, banks don't like that, so it costs you. If abused, banks may even close your accounts.

Savings Account

Your savings account is like your money's secret hideout. This is where you stash the cash you don't need right away. Banks even have withdrawal limits to discourage you from taking out too much.

Whether you're saving up for a big purchase like a car, building an emergency fund (because life happens), or planning that fun spring break trip with your friends, this is the account you need.

The best part? Your money can grow thanks to interest—basically, the bank pays you a little bonus just for keeping your cash with them.

Opening an Account

Most banks offer online services, meaning you can open an account by following the instructions and providing the necessary information via the bank's website or app.

However, I recommend visiting your neighborhood branch and meeting with a bank representative. You can ask them important questions about minimum balances required, withdrawal limits, monthly or transaction fees, ATM fees, and the ability to set up automatic payments or transfers between accounts. They can tell you about new products that may perfectly cater to your age group and needs.

Other Banking Products and Services

Banks and financial institutions offer a variety of products and services beyond just checking and savings accounts. Here is a starter list to get your feet wet on these concepts:

- **Time deposits (Certificates of Deposit or CDs):** Imagine locking away a fixed amount of money for a period, like a year or two, with a guaranteed interest rate. CDs usually offer higher interest rates than regular savings accounts, but you can't touch it during that time.
- **Investment accounts:** These accounts allow you to invest in the stock market. We'll dig into investments in the next chapter.
- **Credit cards:** These cards allow you to borrow up to a specific approved limit to make purchases or withdraw cash. But here is the catch: interests and fees are associated with them. So, they definitely come with strings attached!

- **Loans:** Need a big purchase like a car, college fees, or even a house? Loans work similarly to credit cards but usually for more significant amounts. Banks offer various loan types—each comes with its own interest rates and repayment terms, so ensure you understand all the details before signing the dotted line.
- **Insurance products:** Banks may also offer insurance products like life, health, and property. These products provide financial protection against unexpected events, giving you peace of mind.

Credit: The Good, The Bad, and The Ugly

Ah, credit. It's a tricky beast. On the one hand, credit (loans) can be your golden ticket to more expensive needs—like paying for education or buying a home—not what you impulsively want. It's also a great way to build your credit score. On the other hand, if not used wisely, it can eat you like a monster.

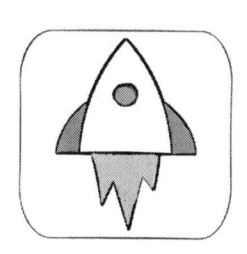

Imagine you spend $200 worth of credit to buy a pair of designer jeans you've been eyeing. It sounds fantastic, but if you don't pay the entire balance when due (usually within a month), you're charged interest that you must pay back on top of the original amount. So, $200 can quickly turn into $240 or more if not properly managed. Ouch, right? This is a perfect example of an impulsive "want."

The rule is: if you can't afford it now, will you be able to afford it for more later? The answer is simple: don't buy it! Or wait until you save enough to afford it without paying interest.

The name of the game is controlling the emotional rush from immediate gratification. Instead, making rational decisions to purchase when you can afford the items is vital.

What Is a Credit Score?

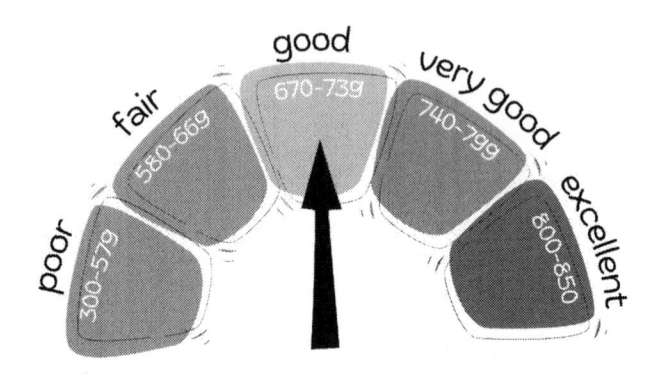

CREDIT SCORE

(poor 300-579, fair 580-669, good 670-739, very good 740-799, excellent 800-850)

A credit score is a magical number that shows lenders (banks, financial institutions, landlords, insurance companies, etc.) how trustworthy you are with borrowed money. Do you pay on time? What does your credit history say about you? Can you afford additional credit?

A person's credit score is between 300 and 850 in the US. The higher your score, the easier it is to get approved for loans, get approval on that apartment lease, snag the best interest rates, and even pay less for car insurance.

To build up a good credit score and move the needle to the right, follow this advice:

- **Pay your bills on time.** Late payments can significantly and negatively impact your credit score. Setting up automatic payments or reminders can ensure you stay on track.
- **Keep your credit card balances low.** Aim to use less than 30% of your available credit. For example, if your credit card has a $1,000 spending limit, don't charge more than $300 until you pay off your previous month's total balance.

- **Pay off balances.** Aim to pay off your credit card balances monthly to boost your score and avoid paying interest or keeping them low.
- **Keep old accounts open to lengthen your credit history.** They can help maintain a more extended credit history even if you use them sparingly. Just make sure there are no unnecessary hidden fees.
- **Avoid opening too many new accounts frequently.** Each time you apply for a new credit card or loan, it triggers a hard inquiry on your credit report, which can slightly lower your score.
- **Have a mix of credit types (e.g., credit cards, auto loans, student loans).** However, don't take out unnecessary loans just to diversify your credit.

The Credit Monster

High interest rates are like the Credit Monster's sharp claws when you borrow money. They can dig deep into your finances, leaving you bleeding money every month. And if you're only making minimum payments on your credit card balance? That's like inviting the Credit Monster to move in with you.

You charge a $1,000 shopping spree with a 20% interest rate on your credit card. If you only make the minimum payment of $25 per month, it'll take you over six years to pay off that balance. And the real kicker? You'll end up shelling out an extra $979 in interest. That's like paying double for everything you bought!

But the Credit Monster's tricks don't stop there. It loves to tempt you with shiny new purchases, promising instant gratification while hiding the long-term costs. It can also demolish your credit score, leaving a path of destruction. Every missed payment and maxed-out card are like giant scratches on your financial reputation, lowering your credit score.

So, how do you fight back? Simple: treat credit like a tool, not a toy. Only use it for needs (not wants) you can't afford upfront, ensuring the expenditure aligns with your values and goals. Always have a solid plan to pay it off ASAP. Pay your bills on time, keep your balances in check, and don't bite off more than you can chew.

Interest Rates: A Two-Way Street

Interest rates are like a two-way street in the world of finance. They can work in your favor when you're saving or investing money, but they can also work against you when you're borrowing (credit cards and loans).

So, when are interest rates your best friend? When you're saving or investing, of course! Let's say you've got some cash in a savings account or invested in the stock market. This cash will generate something extra on top of your original money. It's like getting a bonus just for being smart with your cash.

For example, imagine you've got $1,000 chilling in a savings account that earns 3% interest per year. After a year, you'll have an extra $30 in your pocket without lifting a finger. And the higher the interest rate, the more moola you can rake in over time. Cha-ching!

On the flip side, when you borrow money, like taking out a loan or using a credit card, you pay interest to the lender, as we discussed previously. In America, typical credit card interest rates average 20%, even higher for teens! The higher the interest rate, the more expensive it is to borrow money.

Here's a simple rule of thumb: when saving or investing, you want to hunt down the highest interest rates to score the most bang for your buck. But when you're borrowing, you want to keep those interest rates as low as possible to avoid getting burned or even eaten by the Credit Monster.

Understanding how interest rates work on both sides of the equation can help you make smarter financial decisions and keep more money in your pocket.

Saving, Not Borrowing

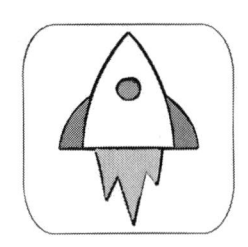

We all have that one big thing we're dreaming of. But how do you turn that dream into a reality without drowning in debt? Whether you're eyeing a once-in-a-lifetime adventure, a new laptop, or the keys to your first car, the secret sauce is simple: **saving up.**

Now, I know what you might be thinking—saving sounds about as fun as watching paint dry. But hear me out! When you try to save for something special, the satisfaction of finally clicking "add to cart" is unbeatable. Knowing you earned it fair and square, you'll savor that purchase, and it's paid off!

Saving is your ticket to getting what you want without the stress of owing money or getting slapped with crazy interest rates. And the best part? It's totally doable, even if you're not a math wizard. Here's how to make it happen:

- **Set a clear goal.** Do you want to save $1,000 for a road trip next summer? Write it down and make it official.
- **Break it down.** Divide your goal amount by the number of weeks or months you must save. $100 per month for ten months? Bam, you've got a plan!
- **Open a separate savings account.** This will separate your goal money from your everyday cash (your checking account), so you're not tempted to dip into it for that late-night pizza craving.
- **Automate it.** Set up automatic transfers from your checking account to your savings account every payday. What you don't see, you won't miss!
- **Cut back on extras.** Skip the daily latte or weekly takeout and watch your savings grow faster than your coffee addiction.
- **Get creative.** Sell your old stuff, take on a side hustle, or put any extra cash (birthday money or tax refund, anyone?) straight into your savings.

But wait, there's more! While rocking your saving habits, remember to build an emergency fund. A safety net of 3–6 months' worth of expenses can be a real lifesaver when unexpected costs pop up, like a car repair or an unexpected visit from your lifelong friend, losing your job, or switching careers. Make intelligent long-term decisions.

For instance, create an emergency fund for unexpected expenses if you have a pet. That way, if ever they get sick or need emergency treatment, you won't have to worry about where the money will come from. It feels good to be fully prepared for emergencies at times like this. The last thing you want when life gets tough is to have to worry about money!

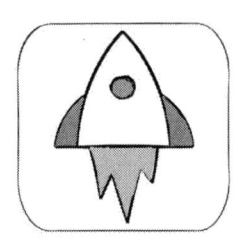

Income: Cash Coming In

The easiest way to get rid of debt and spend on things you want is by earning more money. It's as simple as that!

There are many ways to start earning money in your teen years:

- Part-time gigs at restaurants, coffee shops, or pet stores
- Summer jobs and internships
- Side hustles like babysitting, dog-walking, or house-sitting
- Entrepreneurial ventures like pressure-washing, freelancing or digital marketing
- Sharing your smarts by tutoring kids or helping them with homework
- Your monthly allowance, birthday, and special occasion gifts
- Starting a social media channel or blog

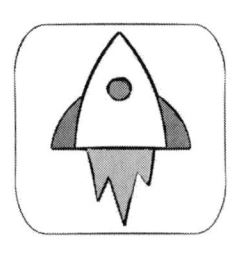

Expenses: Money Going Out

Now, let's talk about the other side of the equation: your expenses. This includes everything you spend your hard-earned cash on (or your parents'). Here's a starter list to help you brainstorm:

- Dining out and entertainment
- Hobbies and sports
- Pet expenses (food, grooming, vet)
- School supplies and textbooks
- Car expenses (gas, insurance, maintenance, tolls)
- Phone bills
- Clothes and gadgets
- Socializing with friends
- Gaming and online subscriptions
- Beauty and self-care (hello, mani-pedis!)
- Healthcare (health insurance, gym memberships)
- School loans or tuition
- Home expenses (rent, utilities, groceries, renters' insurance)
- Vacations
- Giving to charity or causes you care about

- Saving for future purchases or building an emergency fund
- Investment contributions to "Future You"
- Loan and credit card payments
- Computers and/or other technological needs
- Taxes, oh yes, those too!

Keep an eye on where your money is going so you can make informed decisions and adjustments as needed.

Can you identify which expenses classify as 'needs' and 'wants' from the above list?

Budgeting: Your Money's Game Plan

All right, it's time to talk about the "B" word: budgeting. I know, I know—it doesn't exactly scream "fun." Budgeting is a simple way to keep track of your income (the money rolling in) and your expenses (the money flying out). By seeing it all laid out in front of you, you can make sure you're covering your needs, saving for your wants, and not going overboard on those "treat yourself" moments.

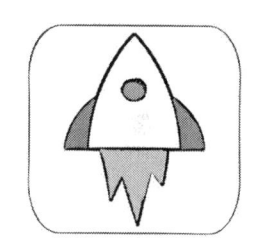

Building Your Budget

Now that you know all the elements of the budget equation: income and expenses, here's a step-by-step guide to building your very own budget. For each category, calculate the monthly amount:

- **Income** (cash coming in).

  ○ **List your income.** Jot down all the money coming in, whether from a part-time job, allowance, or those clever side hustles.

- **Expenses** (cash going out).

  ○ **Track your spending.** Write down everything you spend money on, from the essentials like phone, food, and transportation to the fun stuff like concerts and dining out.
  To make it even easier, budgeting apps are available. Pay for everything via your mobile or card. These apps link to your bank account, giving you a complete list of monthly spending. This

makes it easy to identify things you overspent on. You may not realize how much drinking a gourmet coffee daily can add up to by the end of the month.

  ○ **Set aside savings and investments.** List all your monthly savings and investment contributions. Whether it's for that fun trip, emergency fund, or retirement.

  ○ **Paying down your debt.** Keep tabs on any debts, like student loans or car payments. List the monthly payments to bring those debts down ASAP.

- **Do the math.** Subtract your expenses from your income. If you've got some money left over, give yourself a high-five—that's your surplus! If you're in the red (negative number), don't panic. It just means it's time to make some adjustments.
- **Tweak as needed.** If you're overspending in one area, look for ways to cut back expenses or find creative ways to earn additional income.

Keeping It Simple

The 50/30/20 Rule is like the "easy button" of budgeting. It breaks down your after-tax income into Needs, Wants, and Savings/Debt Repayment. How It Works:

- **50% on needs:** Half of your income goes toward the essentials, like rent, utilities, groceries, phone, education, and transportation. These are nonnegotiable expenses that keep your life running smoothly.
- **30% on wants:** A third of your income is for the fun stuff—dining out, entertainment, hobbies, gaming, giving to causes you care for, and all those little extras that make life enjoyable. Think of it as your "treat yourself" fund.
- **20% on savings or debt repayment:** The remaining 20% is dedicated to your future self. This includes saving, investing for the long haul, and paying off debts faster than a speeding bullet.

The beauty of the 50/30/20 Rule is that it's a simple framework for managing your finances without tracking every dollar! It balances between immediate expenses and future financial goals. It encourages financial discipline while still allowing for enjoyment and quality of life.

The Bottom Line: Money Management Is a Life Skill

Mastering how to handle your money is like acquiring any other skill—it takes practice, patience, and a willingness to make mistakes and grow from them. But the payoff is so worth it. When you're in control of your finances, you're in control of your life in ways you might not have imagined:

- Reduced stress and anxiety
- Improved relationships
- Greater freedom and flexibility
- Increased self-confidence
- Better physical and mental health
- Ability to pursue passions

The key message is to start keeping track of your money and directing it with intention based on your values and goals, not just your bank balance and emotions.

Now that we've covered the basics let's dive deeper. In the next chapter, we'll explore how to make your money work for you through the power of investing and compound interest. Trust me, your future self will thank you. Let's go!

TEN

Growing Your Money

> *It's not how much money you make, but how much money you keep and how hard it works for you.*
>
> Robert Kiyosaki

You're scrolling through your feed, drooling over their latest designer haul or dreamy vacation pics. It's easy to fall into the trap of thinking that more money equals more happiness. But the truth is, chasing material things and trying to keep up with others' highlight reels can leave you feeling unfulfilled and stuck on a never-ending treadmill. "If only I had more money, I'd be happy too." But here's the truth: money should never be the ultimate goal. It's just a tool to help you create the life you want.

This chapter will explore cultivating a healthy money mindset, investing basics, and compound interest's power. We'll also bust some common myths about investing and give you practical tips to start growing your wealth, no matter where you're starting from.

Money Mindset: A Balanced Approach

Rather than chasing after what others have or fitting in with people's expectations, focus on what truly matters to you. What are your dreams, your passions, your goals? Remember those discovery exercises earlier on? Keep them handy. Shifting your perspective from acquiring things to experiencing life on your own terms can lead to a more satisfying and financially healthy existence.

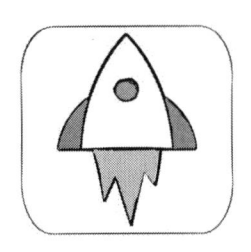

Living within your means isn't about deprivation; it's about making conscious choices that align with your long-term aspirations. Likewise, embracing financial wisdom isn't about hoarding every penny out of fear. It's about finding equilibrium to enjoy life's pleasures without compromising your financial future. Speaking of the future, let's dive into how you can make your money work for you in the long run.

Buckle up because we're about to dive into the world of investing!

Planting The Seeds of Wealth

Money doesn't grow on trees, but it can definitely grow! It's called investing… imagine making all the right moves, so much so that you can lie on a sunny beach while your money grows on its own. Warren Buffett hit the nail on the head when he said, "If you don't find a way to make money while you sleep, you will work until you die."—Warren Buffett.

If you think you're too young to start investing. Think again!

Your Own Money Tree

Investing is similar to growing a garden because it takes patience, care, and anticipation. However, the good news is that even if you start with a small amount, you can start growing your money without delay. So, what do you need to start an investment garden that'll grow your money?

- **Starting Capital = Seeds:** Just as you start a garden by planting seeds, investing begins with an initial capital, also called principal. These seeds represent your initial investment (money) to purchase stocks, bonds, mutual funds, or other instruments available in the market.
- **Investment Growth = Plant Growth:** The growth of your investments can be likened to the growth of plants in your garden. Over time, with the right conditions (market environment), care (strategic management), and patience, your investments can grow just like plants do. Some investments grow

faster (like vegetables) but might be short-lived. In contrast, others grow slower (like trees) but can provide shade and benefits for longer.
- **Diversification = Variety of Plants:** Just as a well-balanced garden has a variety of plants to ensure yield regardless of the seasons, a well-diversified investment portfolio contains a carefully selected mix of investments to protect against market volatility (ups and downs). This way, if one type of investment doesn't perform well, you have others that might still thrive.
- **Market Volatility = Weather Conditions:** The unpredictability of market conditions can be compared to changing weather in gardening. Just as storms, droughts, and changing seasons affect plant growth, the market will also have ups and downs. The key is to stay the course and keep nurturing your investments, even during the storms, by anticipating and adapting to these changes.
- **Compound Interest = Pollination:** Compound interest is when your investment earns interest, and then that interest earns interest, and so on. It's like when you plant one flowering plant in your garden, and bees feed on its flowers, spreading the pollen. Before you know it, you have many more flowering plants than you initially did. Over time, this compounding effect can lead to significant growth.

See the example in the graph below, which shows how compound interest significantly outperforms simple interest over time.
An initial $10,000 investment grows over 50 years:
   *At 5% annual **compound interest**, it grows to $114,674*
   *At 5% annual **simple interest**, it grows to $35,000*

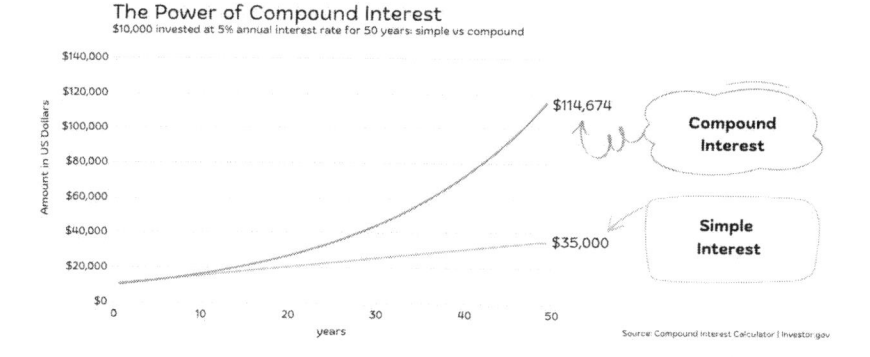

The Power of Compound Interest
$10,000 invested at 5% annual interest rate for 50 years: simple vs compound

Compound Interest: $114,674
Simple Interest: $35,000

Source: Compound Interest Calculator | Investor.gov

- **Consistent Contributions = Expanding Your Garden:** Just like a gardener will want to keep buying new seeds to boost garden expansion and growth, the same principle applies to investments. One of the secrets to achieving exponential growth is adding a monthly contribution to your investment account, even if it's $50 or $100 every month. When you combine the effects of compound interests plus consistent contribution, the gains for your future self are mind-blowing.

The graph below illustrates how regular contributions dramatically boost long-term investment growth.
  Over 40 years at 7% annual compound interest:
   Scenario 1: $10,000 initial + $0 monthly = $149,745
   Scenario 2: $0 initial + $200 monthly = $479,124
   Scenario 3: $10,000 initial + $200 monthly = $628,869

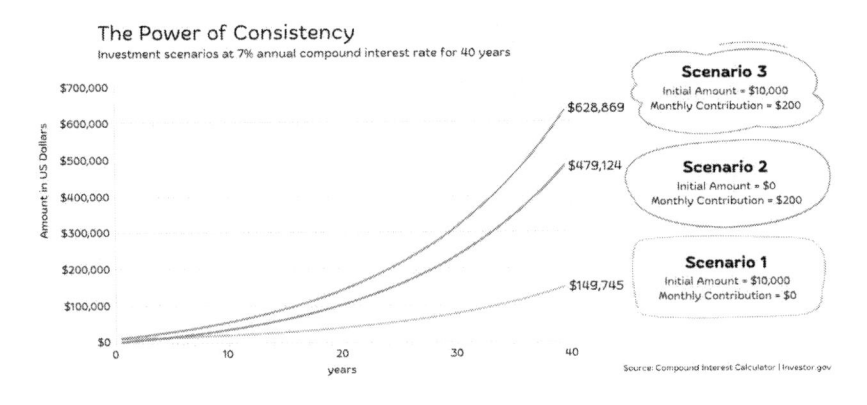

The Power of Consistency
Investment scenarios at 7% annual compound interest rate for 40 years

Scenario 3 — Initial Amount = $10,000, Monthly Contribution = $200 → $628,869
Scenario 2 — Initial Amount = $0, Monthly Contribution = $200 → $479,124
Scenario 1 — Initial Amount = $10,000, Monthly Contribution = $0 → $149,745

Source: Compound Interest Calculator | Investor.gov

- **Tax-Deferred Growth = Protected Greenhouse:** Imagine having a greenhouse that protects your plants from animals or harsh weather, allowing them to grow faster. Some investment accounts, like retirement accounts (e.g., IRAs and 401(k)s), offer tax-deferred growth in America. This means you only pay taxes on the earnings from your investments once you withdraw the money, allowing your investments to grow more rapidly over time.

For example, by investing in a 401(k), your money can compound tax-free for decades, giving you a bigger harvest when you retire. Remember that while tax-deferred accounts offer significant benefits, there are often restrictions on when and how money can be withdrawn without penalties.

- **Patience and Long-Term Perspective = Gardening Seasons:** Successful gardening and investing both require patience and a long-term perspective. Just as you can't rush the growth of a tree or expect immediate harvests, investments typically need time to mature and yield substantial returns. Avoid the shiny objects and the hype over those super-fast, high-return promises. Those are usually tied to a very high degree of risk. But what is investment risk? Let's dive in.
- **Risk Management = Pest Control and Weeding:** Just as gardeners must protect their plants from pests and weeds that may kill them, investors must also manage risks. High risk can lead to high rewards, but it also means a higher chance of losing money—sometimes all of it!

For example, investing in a trendy new tech startup may have the potential to offer huge returns if the company succeeds. Still, it could also fail and result in a total investment loss. Ouch! On the other hand, investing in established companies like Microsoft or Amazon is safer but might grow your money more slowly.

Effective risk management involves a diversified and balanced approach to steadily protect and increase wealth. Don't worry; there are tons of investment products out there that can do that for you!

Now that you understand the basics of investing and how it can help your money grow, it's time to start planting your seeds of wealth. Take a moment to reflect on your financial goals and dreams. What do you want to achieve in the short term (for instance, saving for a down payment on a car) and long-term (like building a nest egg for retirement)? Consider your risk tolerance, too. Are you comfortable with the possibility of higher returns but a higher risk (potentially losing every penny), or do you prefer a slower, steadier approach?

Once you have a clearer picture of your goals and risk profile, explore the investment options available. Remember, even small, consistent contributions can make a big difference over time, thanks to the power of compound interest. So, don't wait—start taking action today and watch your financial garden grow.

Question What You Know

Before we go deeper into the topic of investing and action items, let's address some common misconceptions and excuses that might be holding you back from getting started:

- **"I don't have enough money."** You don't need to be Richie Rich to begin investing. Even small amounts can grow over time with the power of compound interest. In fact, many investment platforms now offer low minimum balance requirements or even fractional shares, making it easier than ever to begin with small amounts of money. The key is to start as early as possible and remain consistent. Even modest monthly contributions like $50 or $100 can grow significantly. If you are under eighteen, ask a parent or guardian to help you. There are apps designed for young people, enabling you to start with just $5.
- **"I don't know enough about the stock market."** Investing may initially seem intimidating, but you don't need to be a financial expert to get started. One beginner-friendly option is exchange-traded funds (ETFs), baskets of investments traded on the stock exchange. ETFs offer instant diversification and lower fees than actively managed funds (stocks you must buy in numerous individual transactions). Other easy-to-understand options include index funds. What is an index fund? An Index groups stocks, bonds, or other securities.

An excellent example of an index is the S&P 500, which includes the 500 largest publicly traded companies in the US. You cannot invest directly in an index, but you can invest in an index fund. This fund buys shares of stock in all the S&P 500 companies, so it mirrors the performance of the S&P 500.

The graph below shows the S&P 500 index fund's performance since inception, with an average annual return of about 10%. This illustrates the potential long-term growth of a diversified index fund investment.
Disclaimer: *Past performance does not guarantee future results. While historical data provides insight, investment returns can vary and may be lower or higher in the future.*

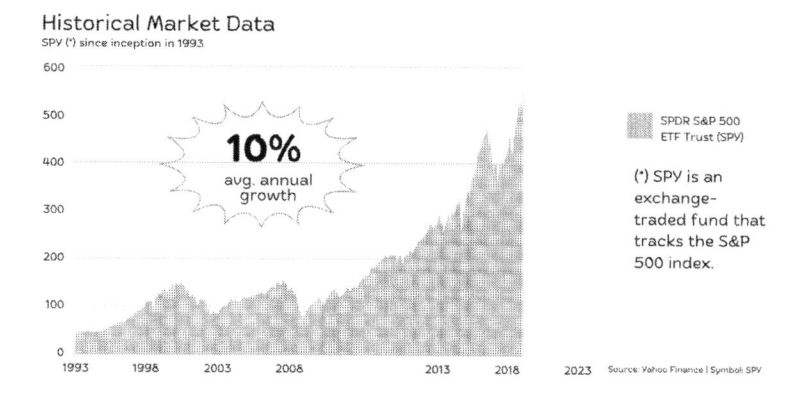

Historical Market Data
SPY (*) since inception in 1993

10% avg. annual growth

SPDR S&P 500 ETF Trust (SPY)

(*) SPY is an exchange-traded fund that tracks the S&P 500 index.

Source: Yahoo Finance | Symbol: SPY

- **"It can wait until I'm older."** This is a common misconception. The truth is the earlier you start investing, the more time your money has to grow through the power of compound interest. Let's look at a clear example.

The graph below shows the benefits of investing early. A monthly $100 investment at 7% annual compound interest until retirement at age 65:
  Starting at 18, you'd retire with $407,744
  Starting at 25, you'd retire with $247,248
  Starting at 35, you'd retire with $116,990

This example clearly highlights how starting to invest just a few years earlier can lead to significantly larger returns over time. By starting at 18 instead of 25, an additional $8,400 in contributions results in an extra $160,496 at retirement - nearly tripling the total retirement savings!

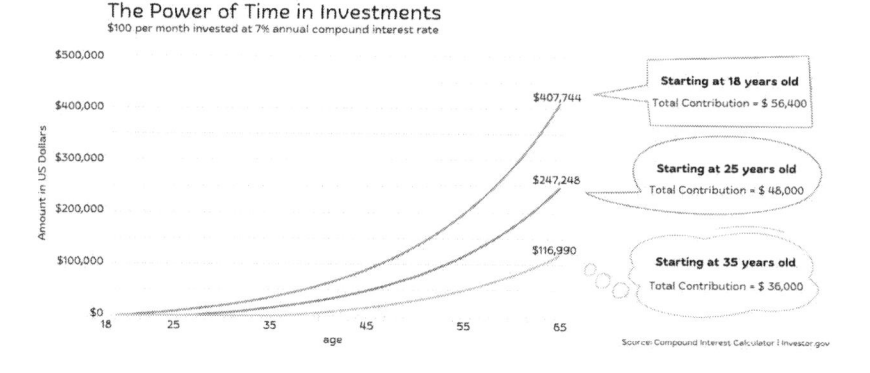

The Power of Time in Investments
$100 per month invested at 7% annual compound interest rate

Starting at 18 years old — Total Contribution = $56,400 — $407,744
Starting at 25 years old — Total Contribution = $48,000 — $247,248
Starting at 35 years old — Total Contribution = $36,000 — $116,990

Source: Compound Interest Calculator | Investor.gov

So, don't wait—start investing as soon as possible, even if it's just a tiny amount each month.

- **"I need to time the market just right."** Trying to predict the perfect time to buy or sell stocks without much knowledge and experience is difficult, stressful, and unnecessary for most long-term investors. Leave that to the professional technical analysts or financial advisers.

  Instead of trying to time the market, focus on consistently investing over time, regardless of short-term fluctuations. This strategy, known as dollar-cost averaging (DCA), helps smooth out the effects of market volatility and ensures that you're investing when prices are both high and low.

- **"I don't have time to invest."** Investing doesn't have to be a time-consuming process. By setting up automatic contributions to your investment accounts, you can make investing a hassle-free part of your financial routine. Most investment platforms and employers offering retirement plans allow you to set up automatic transfers so you can invest consistently without thinking about it.

Now that we've addressed these common objections, it's time to take action. Starting is the most crucial step, even if you're starting small. Don't let fear or doubt hold you back—start planting the seeds of your financial success today!

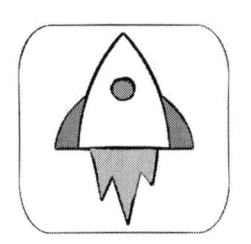

The Magic Formula

Albert Einstein once called compound interest "the eighth wonder of the world" and "the most powerful force in the universe."

Compound interest is the interest you earn on your initial investment (those seeds) plus the interest earned on your previous interest. Over time, this snowball effect can cause your wealth to grow exponentially, even if you start with a relatively small amount. Refer to the graphs in the previous section. It's like planting a single seed that grows into a tree, producing more seeds, which grow into more trees, and so on.

To take advantage of the power of compound interest, there are four key ingredients you need to include in your investment strategy:

Time

The longer your money stays invested, the more time it has to grow through the power of compound interest, so start early, even if you only have a small amount to invest. Experts say the best time to start investing is yesterday, and the second best is today!

Consistency

By contributing a fixed amount to your investment accounts each month, you can take advantage of dollar-cost averaging, which helps smooth out the effects of short-term market fluctuations. It is also a healthy habit of setting money aside for your future self.

Diversity

Choosing well-diversified, low-cost investment products, such as index funds or ETFs, can help you achieve a diversified portfolio that aligns with your goals and risk tolerance. These products spread your money across various investments, reducing exposure to one company or industry.

Patience

Investing is a long-term game, and staying the course is essential, even during market downturns. Trust your investment strategy and give your portfolio the time it needs to recover and grow.

By combining these four elements—time, consistency, diversified investment products, and patience—with the catalyst of compound interest, you'll be well on your way to achieving your financial goals and creating a safety net for your future.

Investing vs. Speculating

It's important to note that this magic formula is based on a long-term investing approach, not short-term speculation.

Investing is like planting an oak tree—it takes time, nurturing, and patience to see it grow into a mighty giant.

Speculating, on the other hand, is more like betting on which acorn will sprout the fastest. It might be exciting in the short term, but it's not a reliable strategy for building lasting wealth.

Remember, slow and steady wins the race when it comes to investing. By combining time, consistency, diversified investment products, and patience with the power of compound interest, you'll be well on your way to achieving your financial dreams and creating a life of abundance and freedom.

Don't be sucked into the latest fad in the markets because you heard that your brother's friend made sums of money quickly. There might be something there, but be curious and only put up that amount of money you are willing to lose entirely. This is speculating, like going to the casino—you could win, but the odds are not in your favor.

Instead, turn those odds in your favor with highly reliable, time-tested tools and practices. By starting early, being consistent, investing in a diversified product, and staying patient, you will succeed and succeed big over time.

Seeking Guidance and Taking Action

All right, you're pumped about investing and ready to watch your money multiply like gremlins. But where do you start? Don't worry—you don't have to do it alone. Plenty of resources are out there to help you navigate the investing world.

First things first: educate yourself. You don't have to become a financial expert overnight, but it helps to understand some basic concepts.

If you're in college, see if your school offers finance classes. Even if it's not your major, taking an elective can give you a solid foundation. Also, there are plenty of online courses available. Because investment is crucial for your financial future, embrace as many opportunities as possible to learn more about it.

Feel free to tap into your personal network. Ask your parents, mentors, or family friends if they have any experience with investing. They might have some sage wisdom to share or know a financial adviser they may recommend who can help you get started.

Regarding financial advisers, if you go that route, look for a certified financial planner (CFP) or a registered investment adviser (RIA) who can help you create a personalized plan based on your goals and risk tolerance. Just ensure they're legit—check their credentials and read reviews before handing over your hard-earned cash.

When you're ready to take the plunge, there are a few key things to consider:

- **Tax implications:** Different types of investment accounts (like 401(k)s, IRAs, and regular brokerage accounts) have different tax rules. Some let you invest pre-tax money, while others make you pay taxes upfront. Do your homework to find the best option for your situation.
- **Rate of return:** This is the percentage your investment earns over time. Higher-risk investments tend to have higher potential returns, while lower-risk investments tend to have lower returns. It's all about finding the right balance for your goals and timeline.
- **Inflation:** This is the enemy of savers everywhere. When inflation goes up, your money loses value over time. That's why keeping all your cash in a low-interest savings account is like watching your purchasing power slowly die.

Imagine you have $10, and you love buying candy bars. Since each candy bar costs $1 today, you can buy ten candy bars with your $10.

Now, let's fast forward to next year. Due to inflation, the prices of things, including candy bars, have gone up. So, instead of $1, each candy bar now costs $1.10.

With the same $10, you can only buy nine candy bars instead of ten because the price has increased. This means your money doesn't stretch as far as it used to. Even though you have the same amount of money, it has less buying power because prices have increased.

This is precisely why investing is important—it helps your money grow faster than inflation, so you can maintain or even increase your buying power over time. This cannot happen if you leave your money in your savings account growing at 3% when inflation is as high as 5% or 10%, for example.

- **Types of investment accounts:** Many options exist, from retirement to health savings accounts to college savings plans. Each has its own rules and benefits, so do your research to find the best fit for your needs.

- **Types of investment instruments:** Stocks, bonds, mutual funds, oh my! There are many different ways to invest your money, each with its own level of risk and potential reward. If you're just starting out, consider a low-cost index fund or a target-date retirement fund that automatically adjusts your investments as you age.
- **Employer matching:** If you're lucky enough to have a job that offers a 401(k) or other retirement plan, grab it with both hands and take advantage of any employer matching. It's free money and can add up big time over the years.

Remember, investing is a marathon, not a sprint. It's all about consistency, patience, and a long-term mindset. So, start planting those money seeds now, and watch your wealth grow over time. Your future self will give you a big old bear hug for taking control of your finances early on.

Money Matters

Money management is an ongoing journey. Use these tools regularly to refine your understanding and stay true to your evolving self:

Journal Prompts

- Write about a recent financial decision. What influenced your choice? What would you do differently next time?
- Reflect on your current relationship with money. What would you like to change?

Action Items

- Track your monthly spending, categorizing each expense as need and want.
- Review your credit report and score. Identify areas for improvement.
- Create a plan to pay off any existing debt.
- Research and list three potential side hustles you could start.
- Develop an "emergency fund" savings plan.
- Open an investment account.

- Set up automatic transfers to your savings and investment accounts.

Interactive Activities

- **Budget challenge:** Create a mock monthly budget using the 50/30/20 rule. Adjust it for different income levels.
- **Investment simulator:** Use an online stock market simulator to practice investing without real money.
- **Compound interest calculator:** Experiment with different saving scenarios using an online compound interest calculator.
- **Financial goal vision board:** Create a visual representation of your financial goals.

Expand Your Money Matters Toolkit

Scan the QR code below to access bonus resources, including worksheets, templates, videos, recommended tools, apps, online calculators, and additional money management tips. Check back often for updates and fresh content.

The Compass Points to Financial Independence

Now that you have the tools to take care of your finances, let's move on to the next and final part of this book—taking care of yourself from the inside out. Because let's be honest, all the money in the world won't matter if you're not healthy and fully functional.

So, we've covered North, East, South, and West. Your compass is nearly complete! You've learned about discovering your passions, honing your skills, growing your mindset, strengthening your circle of trust, and mastering your money. But one crucial element holds everything together —you, a healthy you!

Part Five: Center

VIBE CHECK

The Wellness Warriors: *Embracing the mind-body-soul connection, these personas cultivate balance in all aspects of life. They prioritize physical health, mental well-being, and spiritual growth, understanding that life fulfillment involves a holistic nurturing of self.*

ELEVEN

Reaching Peak Health

> *Take care of your body. It's the only place you have to live.*
>
> Jim Rohn

You might have all the money in the world, the most extraordinary squad, and a dream career lined up, but what's the point if you're not taking care of yourself? It's like having a shiny Ferrari (a.k.a. your body) but forgetting to fuel it properly. You look fabulous in the driver's seat but won't get far on an empty tank! That's why we've saved the best for last— your health!

Ready to unlock your ultimate power hack? Buckle up because we're about to dive into the good stuff!

Youth Isn't Immunity

Yes, you aren't immune, but it feels like it sometimes! We've all been there. Scarfing down junk food like there's no tomorrow, pulling all-nighters, driving carelessly 20 miles above the speed limit, or rolling out eyes at mom's lectures about "making good choices." Sound familiar?

It's easy to feel invincible when you're young. Your body bounces back fast, and consequences seem like a problem for Future You. But here's the thing: just because you can't see the damage doesn't mean it's not happening.

Here's a mind-bender: Your brain is still figuring things out. Neuroscientist and professor Dr. Gary Wenk (2010) explains that the teenage brain is still developing myelination. It's like your brain's built-in "consequences calculator." Without your brain entirely online and engaged, it's prone to do risky stuff without realizing the potential fallout.

Reality Check

Did you know that the majority of leading causes of death in America are actually preventable? We're talking about heart disease, cancer, stroke, respiratory illnesses, diabetes — the big, scary stuff that we all hope to avoid. Here's the kicker: a whopping 40% of premature deaths can be chalked up to unhealthy behaviors like smoking, poor diet, lack of physical activity, and substance abuse. It's all about choices!

The tricky part? These chronic diseases often feel like distant, abstract threats — something that happens to "other people" or in some far-off future. It's easy to dismiss them with a casual "That won't happen to me" or "I'll worry about that later." After all, when you're young and feeling invincible, the idea of heart disease or diabetes can seem as remote as living on Mars.

But here's the reality check: these diseases don't just appear out of nowhere. They're like silent ninjas, developing stealthily over the years, even decades before symptoms become apparent. By the time you notice something's wrong, the groundwork has already been laid. That greasy burger you're eating today? The workout you're skipping? The cigarette or joint you're lighting up? They're all potentially contributing to health issues that you will have to deal with in the future.

The challenge is to bridge that mental gap — to make these seemingly distant health concerns feel relevant and actionable now. It's about realizing that your choices today shape the health landscape you'll inhabit tomorrow. So, while it might not feel urgent or even real right now, giving these potential health issues a second thought today could make all the difference in your future.

Let that sink in for a minute.

But wait, there's more! Just because something's legal doesn't automatically make it safe or smart. Let's break it down:

- **Marijuana:** It is legal in many places, but it can still mess with your developing brain. Regular use in adolescence is linked to impaired

brain development, cognitive (thinking) deficits, lower academic achievement, and increased risk of mental health issues. Not cool at all! Makes you wonder… why is its legality expanding as we speak?
- **Juul and vapes:** Marketed as a "safer" alternative, but still highly addictive and harmful to your lungs. Totally not cool!
- **Alcohol:** Literally poison for your body if abused, even if it's everywhere once you're of age.
- **Sugar:** Totally legal and highly promoted for kids, but too much sugar leads to serious health issues.
- **Prescription opioids:** Doctor-approved doesn't mean risk-free. These can be super addictive and life-threatening if abused.

The point? Your body is way too awesome to experiment on. Don't let Big Corp, politicians, or peer pressure decide what's best for you. Think of yourself as the CEO of You, Inc. – start making choices that benefit your long-term success!

Trend to Dependency

While your brain is still developing, getting caught up in risky behaviors that seem fun without considering long-term consequences is easy. When everyone around you is doing it, it's tempting to join in, thinking it must be okay. They seem to be enjoying themselves, so what's the harm?

One of the most significant temptations is substance use, including alcohol, tobacco, marijuana, opioids, and other drugs.

Here are some shocking statistics (National Center for Drug Abuse Statistics n.d.):

- 62% of 12th graders are alcohol drinkers
- 1 in 5 high school students report current marijuana use
- Opioids (painkillers and heroin) are responsible for 70% of overdose deaths in America
- 75% of teen smokers report cravings
- In 2021, over 900,000 teens reported past-year use of cocaine, over 300,000 used methamphetamine, and around 50,000 used heroin. What?

Substance use can seriously mess with your brain and body, especially during adolescence. Teens who start drinking before the age of 15 are at a higher risk for developing alcohol use disorder (AUD) later in life (National Institute on Alcohol Abuse and Alcoholism 2024). Regular teen drinkers have been shown to have a hippocampus (responsible for memory and learning) that's 10% smaller than non-drinkers. (Robson, 2024).

But it's not just about long-term health risks. Substance use and abuse can lead to immediate, potentially life-altering consequences.

When you're under the influence, your decision-making abilities take a serious hit. Suddenly, getting behind the wheel seems like a good idea, even though you know it's dangerous. You might say things you'd never say sober, hurting relationships or your reputation. You could find yourself in risky situations, making choices that compromise your safety or values.

These substances lower your inhibitions, meaning the smart, 'responsible you' takes a backseat to an impulsive, reckless version of yourself. One night of "fun" could lead to regrets that last a lifetime – whether it's a DUI, a fight you can't take back, or choices that impact your future opportunities.

Healthy vs. Unhealthy Brain SPECT Images

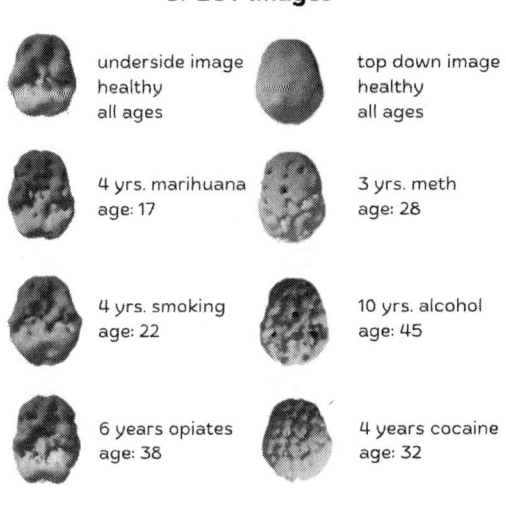

	underside image healthy all ages		top down image healthy all ages
	4 yrs. marihuana age: 17		3 yrs. meth age: 28
	4 yrs. smoking age: 22		10 yrs. alcohol age: 45
	6 years opiates age: 38		4 years cocaine age: 32

Source: AmenClinics.com

If you are still not sure, check out the image above which provides a striking visual representation of how various substances can affect the brain over time, as shown through SPECT imaging. The SPECT (Single Photon Emission Computed Tomography) images below clearly demonstrate the physical impact of substance abuse on the brain, with affected areas appearing as dark spots or holes compared to healthy brain scans (Amen Clinics). These visual representations underscore the urgency of addressing substance abuse, especially among young people whose brains are still developing.

It's a vicious cycle – these substances can feel amazing in the moment. Still, they hijack your brain's reward system, making it harder to feel good without them. Before you know it, you're trapped in addiction.

Remember, we all make mistakes. No one sets out to become addicted. The key is awareness, compassion for yourself and others, and knowing that change is always possible. It's not about perfection; it's about progress.

Should I Seek Help?

If you are wondering if substances are becoming a problem, ask yourself:

- Do you experience withdrawal symptoms when not using?
- Do you need more substance for the same effect (increased tolerance)?
- Have you tried unsuccessfully to cut down or control use?
- Do you continue using despite knowing the harmful consequences?
- Do you spend a lot of time obtaining, using, or recovering from the substance?
- Do you think a lot about it?
- Do you need it to help you have fun with friends?
- Is there a strong desire or urge to use the substance?
- Have you given up important activities and relationships because of substance use?
- Have you noticed significant changes in your personality, such as mood swings, engaging in risky activities, or having less interest in the things you once enjoyed?

If you answered yes to some of these, it's courageous to recognize there might be a problem. Seek help from someone who can walk through it with you, whether a counselor, parent, family member or one of your trusted guides. Breaking an addiction is tough to do alone, but support is always available. Just speak up!

Change Is Possible

> *A year from now, you will wish you had started today.*
>
> Karen Lamb

Habits

We're creatures of habit, and that's not always bad. Habits make life easier and more comfortable. The trick is keeping the good ones and ditching the bad. Here's a quick rundown:

- Good habits can help us and create discipline.
- Bad habits can harm us and create dependency.
- Good habits can be hard to maintain; bad habits are easy to fall into.

Understanding the habit loop can help you break bad habits and form new ones:

- **Cue:** The trigger (seeing a cookie).
- **Routine:** The action (eating a cookie or a whole jar).
- **Reward:** The result (sugar rush).

Making Change Happen

Ready to shake things up? Awesome! But remember, change isn't like flipping a switch. It takes time, effort, and a whole lot of self-compassion.

Fun Fact: It takes an average of 66 days to form a new habit, but it can range from 18 to 254 days. So don't sweat it if it takes a while!

The Six Stages of Change:

1. **Precontemplation:** Not even thinking about changing.
2. **Contemplation:** Starting to acknowledge the issue.
3. **Preparation:** Deciding to change and making a plan.
4. **Action:** Actively working on changing behavior.
5. **Maintenance:** Keeping up the good work.
6. **Lapse/relapse:** Slips happen – how you bounce back matters. Just jump on the wagon again and try again.

Ingredients for Effective Change

If there is something in your life that you would like to change, ensure you embrace the five ingredients of effective change:

- **Set SMART goals:** Having realistic expectations and a well-defined and achievable action plan with specific goals using the SMART technique will serve you well. Concentrate on goals that are:

    - **S**—Specific
    - **M**—Measurable
    - **A**—Achievable
    - **R**—Relevant
    - **T**—Timely

    "I want to be healthier" is too vague. "I will eat five servings of fruits and veggies daily for the next month" is a SMART goal.

    Examples of SMART goals:
    - "I will set up an appointment with my school counselor or therapist to discuss my vaping habit by the end of this week."
    - "I will prepare and eat home-cooked meals at least five nights a week for the next month."
    - "I will exercise for 30 minutes, four days a week, for the next six weeks."
    - "I will establish a consistent sleep schedule for weeknights, going to bed by 10 p.m. and waking up at 6 a.m. for the next two weeks."

- **Motivation:** Connect with your "why." What's driving you to make this change? Is it to feel better physically and mentally? To

set yourself up for a healthier future? It's easier to stay on track when you're connected to your reason.
- **Support:** Build your cheer squad. Surround yourself with people who support your goals and believe in you. They'll celebrate your wins and help you bounce back from setbacks.
- **New lifestyle:** Think long-term. See this change as part of your new lifestyle, not just a temporary fix.
- **Self-compassion:** Embrace your journey, bumps and all. Change is a rollercoaster – exhilarating and scary. Don't beat yourself up when you stumble (and you will). Instead, offer yourself the same kindness you'd give a friend. See every setback as a setup for a comeback.

Remember, progress is progress, no matter how small. Every step counts. If you slip up, don't let it derail you completely. Just get back on track and keep pushing forward.

Practical Tips for Lasting Change

- **Start small:** Break big goals into tiny, manageable steps. Remember the Two-Minute Rule?
- **Track your progress:** Use a habit tracker or journal.
- **Celebrate small wins:** Reward yourself for hitting milestones.
- **Learn from setbacks:** Analyze what went wrong and adjust your approach.
- **Visualize success:** Imagine yourself achieving your goal.
- **Create a supportive environment:** Remove temptations and add positive cues.
- **Be patient:** Remember, lasting change takes time.

The Power of Yet

When you're struggling, add "yet" to your self-talk:

- "I can't do this… yet."
- "I'm not good at this… yet."
- "I haven't reached my goal… yet."

This simple word reminds you that you're on a journey of growth and improvement.

Change isn't always easy, but it's always possible. By understanding how habits work, recognizing the stages of change, and implementing effective strategies, you're setting yourself up for success. It's not about being perfect – continue progressing and becoming your best version.

So, what habit are you ready to change? What's your first small step? The Future You is cheering you on!

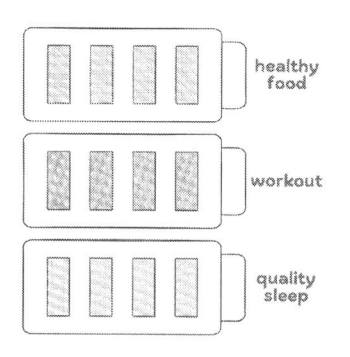

Eat, Move, Thrive

Let's meet the three musketeers of physical health: diet, exercise, and sleep. These guys work together to keep you feeling your best. Again, you don't have to be perfect –finding a balance that works for you is vital.

Diet: Fueling Your Body

What you eat matters—a lot! The Centers for Disease Control and Prevention (Lui 2019) found that one in three kids and teens are overweight or obese, and it's not genetics; it's mainly due to what we eat (and how much of it).

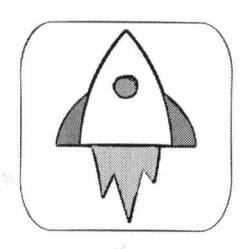

What's My BMI?

Your body mass index (BMI) is a key indicator of health risks. A high BMI can lead to issues like asthma, sleep apnea (when you temporarily stop breathing during sleep), joint and muscle pain, and insulin resistance (sugar running wild inside your body). It can even affect your mental health, self-esteem, and self-confidence (Nemours TeensHealth 2022).

Weight Status	Percentile Range
Underweight	Less than 18.5
Healthy Weight	18.5 – 24.9
Overweight	25.0 – 29.9
Obesity	Equal to or greater than 30.0

Several resources are available to calculate the body mass index (BMI). Scan the QR code in the Wellness Corner at the end of Chapter Thirteen to access our curated list of BMI calculators and other health assessment tools.

Meal Recommendations

- **Portion control:** Ideally, your plate should look something like this:

    o Half filled with vegetables and fruits.
    o Quarter filled with lean proteins.
    o Quarter filled with whole grains.

- **Sugar is your enemy.** Excess sugar in your bloodstream is literally toxic. The damage it causes over time is mind-blowing. Instead of sugary snacks, try:

    o Fresh fruits like apples, berries, oranges for a natural sweet fix.
    o Nuts and seeds such as almonds, walnuts, or pumpkin seeds.
    o Veggies with hummus or guacamole for a savory and filling snack.
    o Greek yogurt with granola and fresh fruit for a protein-packed treat.

- **The right carbs: simple vs complex.** Understanding the difference between simple and complex carbohydrates is crucial for maintaining balanced energy levels and overall health:

    o Simple carbs (e.g., white bread, pasta, sugary snacks, sodas) are quickly digested, causing rapid spikes in blood sugar followed by energy crashes. They often lack essential nutrients.
    o Complex carbs (e.g., whole grains, vegetables, legumes) are digested more slowly, providing sustained energy, and contain more fiber, vitamins, and minerals.

- **Morning carbs are your go-to.** In the morning, fuel up with complex carbs to power through until lunch. Good choices include:

    o Oatmeal topped with fresh fruit and a sprinkle of nuts or seeds.
    o Whole-grain toast with egg and avocado.

○ Protein pancakes with peanut butter.

- **Later in the day, focus on lean proteins and healthy fats.** Some options are:

  ○ Grilled chicken, fish, tofu, or lean beef.
  ○ Lentils, beans, Greek yogurt, or cottage cheese.
  ○ Avocados, nuts, seeds, olive oil, or fatty fish like salmon or tuna.

- **Fuel your muscles.** Don't forget the importance of protein, especially if you're into strength training. Here's the scoop:

  ○ Aim for 20 to 30 grams of protein within 60 minutes after your workout. This helps repair and build muscle.
  ○ Spread your protein intake throughout the day for best results.

- **Hydration is key.** Your body is mostly water, with about 60% of your weight coming from H2O. This isn't just taking up space – water is crucial for nearly every bodily function. The benefits of proper hydration include cellular health, temperature regulation, joint lubrication, digestion, brain function, physical performance, skin, kidney, and other critical organs' health, blood pressure regulation, nutrient absorption, and much more.

To stay hydrated, keep the following tips in mind:
  ○ Drink 2/3 of your weight (lb) in ounces of water daily. For example, if you weigh 150 pounds, 150 pounds × 2/3 = 100 ounces of water per day ~ 8 to 10 glasses daily.
  ○ Increase your water intake when:
    ♦ Exercising (drink an extra 12 oz for every 30 minutes of exercise).
    ♦ In hot or humid climates.
    ♦ You are ill.
    ♦ Traveling, especially by air.
  ○ Start and end your day with a tall glass of water to jumpstart hydration.
  ○ Listen to your body – if you're thirsty, drink water!
  ○ Check your urine color – pale yellow indicates good hydration.

Water is always the best choice, while other beverages count towards fluid intake. It's calorie-free, cost-effective, and readily available. Make staying hydrated a habit.

These simple yet impactful changes to your nutritional habits will give you sustained energy, improved mood, and overall well-being.

Exercise: Get Moving

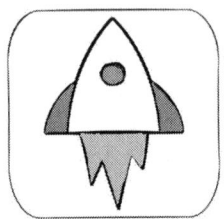

Exercise is vital for all ages and will help you feel physically and mentally fit. Before you start having flashbacks to gym class dodgeball, hear me out. Exercise doesn't have to mean suffering or pumping iron at the gym. It simply involves moving your body in a way that makes you feel good.

Benefits include improved heart health, stronger muscles, better blood sugar control, reduced stress, and a brain boost. Numerous studies have shown that exercising reduces or eliminates stress, anxiety, and even depression.

Our modern lifestyle makes it easy to be sedentary. Teens in America spend an average of 8.5 hours on screens daily for non-study purposes. This is linked to obesity and poor mental health.

Find Your Fit

Getting active doesn't have to feel like a chore. Here are some ways to make exercise fun and effective:

- **Mix it up:** Aim for a combination of cardio and strength training throughout the week.
- **Daily movement:** Try for at least 30 minutes of moderate activity most days. This could be:

    ○ A brisk walk with friends or your dog
    ○ Dancing to your favorite playlist
    ○ Cycling around your neighborhood

- **Heart-pumping action:** 2 to 3 times a week, go for activities that really get your heart rate up, like:

    ○ Playing a sport you enjoy (basketball, soccer, tennis)
    ○ High-intensity interval training (HIIT) workouts
    ○ Swimming laps

- **Strength training:** 2 to 3 times a week, focus on building muscle:

- Bodyweight exercises (push-ups, squats, lunges)
- Resistance band workouts
- Weight training (if you have access to equipment)

- **Join a team:** School sports or community leagues are great for exercise and socializing.
- **Try classes:** Yoga, dance, martial arts – find a class that fits you.
- **Make it social:** Exercise with friends or family to stay motivated.
- **Use tech:** Fitness apps and video games can make working out more engaging.
- **Outdoor adventures:** Hiking, rock climbing, or kayaking can be great weekend activities.
- **Listen to your body:** Start slow and gradually increase intensity. Rest when you need to.

Remember, the best exercise is the one you'll actually do. Find activities you enjoy, and staying active will become a natural part of your lifestyle!

Sleep: Dream On

Last but definitely not least: Sleep. This is like the secret weapon of health that teens usually ignore. But getting enough quality Zs is crucial for everything from your physical health to your mental well-being.

Why is sleep so important? During sleep, your body repairs, processes memories, and regulates hormones. Skimping on sleep can lead to concentration issues, mood swings, anxiety, and weight gain.

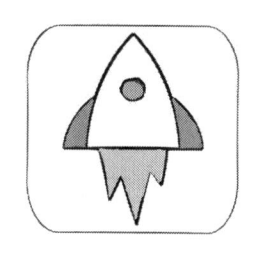

Teens and young adults need 8 to 10 hours of sleep per night. To improve your sleep:

- Develop a relaxing bedtime routine: reading, stretching, taking a warm bath, and sleeping in a dark and quiet room.
- Maintain a consistent sleep schedule.
- Avoid screens 1 to 2 hours before bed. Keeping electronics in another room overnight is helpful to avoid reaching out through the night.
- Use your bed only for sleeping. No homework, electronics, or video games.
- Exercise daily, but preferably not close to bedtime.

- Avoid caffeine after mid-afternoon.
- Take short naps if needed, but not after 3 p.m.

Doing Something About It

We all engage in unhealthy behaviors sometimes. We're human, and we're not perfect. No one sets out to become overweight, addicted, or sedentary, but life happens. The good news is that you can make positive changes. It's not about being flawless—it's about progress in the right direction.

TWELVE

Building Your Mental Fortress

> *Mental health problems don't define who you are. They are something you experience. You walk in the rain and you feel the rain, but, importantly, YOU ARE NOT THE RAIN.*
>
> Matt Haig

Life can be unpredictable sometimes, and feeling stressed, anxious, or down in the dumps is normal. In fact, hundreds of millions of people struggle with mental health challenges, and teens are especially vulnerable. Between peer pressure, body changes, and trying to figure out who you are, it's no wonder that many young people feel overwhelmed.

The good news is that there are ways to cope with these challenges and come out stronger on the other side. That's where Cognitive Behavioral Therapy (CBT) comes in. CBT is like a mental health toolkit to help you understand the connection between your thoughts, feelings, and behaviors.

Embracing Cognitive Behavioral Therapy (CBT)

At its core, CBT is all about becoming aware of how your thoughts, emotions, and behaviors are all interconnected, like a three-legged stool.

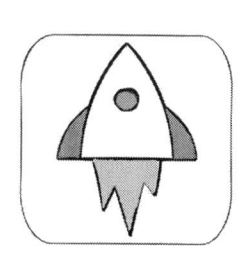

When one leg is wobbly, the whole thing can come crashing down.

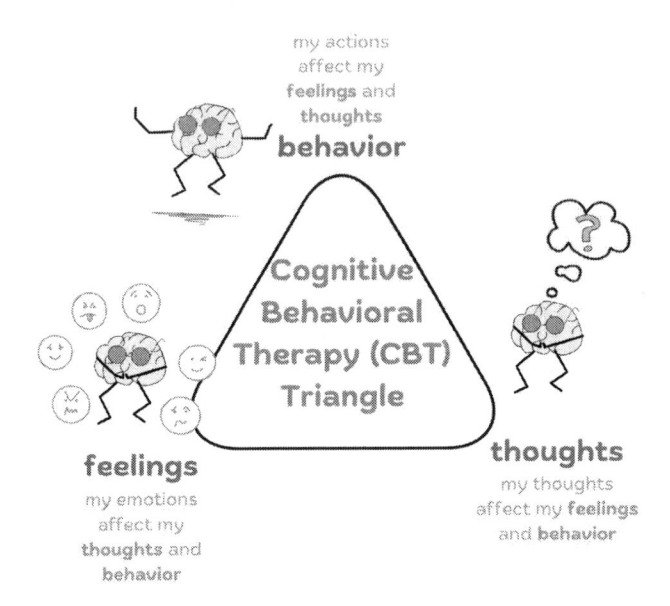

Cognitive Behavioral Therapy (CBT) Triangle

- **behavior**: my actions affect my feelings and thoughts
- **feelings**: my emotions affect my thoughts and behavior
- **thoughts**: my thoughts affect my feelings and behavior

For example, let's say you feel anxious about an upcoming test. You might think, "I'm going to fail," or "I'm not smart enough." These negative **thoughts** can trigger **feelings** of fear and self-doubt, leading to **behaviors** like procrastinating or avoiding studying altogether.

CBT helps you identify and replace these negative thought patterns with more realistic, positive ones. It's not about denying your feelings or pretending everything is sunshine and rainbows. Instead, it's about recognizing and accepting your thoughts while learning to challenge those causing you harm.

All human beings sometimes become consumed by negative thought patterns. Some of the most common patterns that CBT can help with include (Hartney, 2023):

- **Personalization:** Blaming yourself for things that aren't entirely your fault.
- **Magnifying or minimizing:** Blowing things out of proportion or downplaying your achievements.

- **Selective attention:** Focusing only on the negative aspects of a situation.
- **All-or-nothing thinking:** Seeing things as either perfect or a complete failure.
- **Mind reading:** Assuming you know what others are thinking about you.
- **Fortune telling:** Predicting the worst-case scenario without evidence.
- **Blaming:** Holding others responsible for your own emotions or circumstances.
- **Procrastination or avoidance:** Constantly postponing essential tasks, finding excuses to delay difficult conversations or decisions, or engaging in distracting activities to avoid dealing with the issue.
- **Should statements:** Frequently thinking about things you "should" or "must" do.
- **Labeling:** Attaching permanent labels to yourself or others based on single instances of behavior instead of recognizing that one action doesn't define a person's entire character.
- **Personalization or blame:** Blaming yourself or others for a situation involving factors beyond your control.

CBT can help you manage stress, anxiety, and depression by:

- Identifying your triggers and thought patterns.
- Challenging negative thoughts and beliefs with evidence and realistic alternatives.
- Facing your fears gradually through exposure therapy.
- Integrating relaxation techniques like deep breathing or guided imagery into your daily routine.
- Keep an emotions inventory or journal to track your progress.

Thought Reframing Activity

The next time you come across a negative thought like "Nobody likes me," "I'm not smart enough," or "It's all my fault," take your journal and fill in this table. I have provided some sample answers that may inspire you when you wish to complete one yourself. When answering, aim to explain why you feel or think that way:

The thought being questioned is...	For example: "Nobody likes me at school."
What is the evidence for this? Against it?	For instance: Evidence for it: "Sandra didn't invite me to her barbecue." Evidence against it: "My friends ask me out all the time. This is one of the few times I wasn't invited."
Are my thoughts based on facts or feelings?	My thought is based on feelings.
Is this thought black and white, or are things more complicated?	It's complicated because Sandra told me her mom said she could only invite five people.
Could I be making any assumptions or misinterpreting the evidence?	Yes. Sandra and the others could like me. Maybe she wanted to invite the new kid in school, as she has asked me over so many times.
How would other people I know interpret this situation?	My mom and sister would probably not sweat it and just call someone else to spend the day with.
Could my thought be an exaggeration of what is actually happening?	Yes, I am well-liked and have good friends, and Sandra probably did not mean any harm.
Do I habitually think this way?	Yes, sometimes I feel rejected when I am not invited to places.
Did someone pass this thought to me? Are they reliable?	Lily seemed to delight in telling me Sandra was having a party and not inviting me. She said she would be angry if she were in my shoes.
Is my thought a probable scenario or a worst-case scenario?	The thought is a worst-case scenario. Not being invited to a party does not mean nobody likes me at school.

Did you see how answering these questions can help you reframe your thoughts? Now that you understand CBT let's explore some specific mental health challenges and how CBT can help.

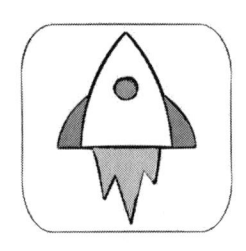

Managing Mental Health Challenges

Mental health challenges like stress, anxiety, and depression are common, especially among teens. Understanding these issues and having strategies to cope with them is crucial for your overall well-being.

Stress

Stress is like the common cold of mental health — everyone deals with it at some point. But just like a cold, it can become harmful if left unchecked. Homework, exams, friend drama, money, and social schedules can become too much, increasing your stress levels.

Here are some effective stress-management techniques:

- **Time management:** One of the biggest causes of stress is not handling deadlines and time properly. Use a planner or app to prioritize tasks and break large projects into smaller, manageable

steps. Check out Chapter Five's section about time management and the Wellness Corner at the end of Chapter Thirteen for bonus resources.
- **Set boundaries:** Learn to say "no" to avoid over-committing yourself.
- **Talk it out:** Sharing your feelings with a trusted friend or adult can help you understand where you are and how to deal with it, and know it's not all on your shoulders.
- **Stay active:** Regular exercise releases pent-up frustration and stress.
- **Thought restructuring:** Challenge stress-inducing thoughts like perfectionism or catastrophizing with more realistic, balanced alternatives (as in the above exercise).
- **Practice mindfulness:** Use deep breathing or meditation to stay present.
- **Get enough sleep:** When you're tired, you get edgy much quicker. Adequate rest helps you handle stress better.
- **Take breaks:** Pushing through can cause burnout and more stress. Regular short breaks are recommended.

Anxiety

Anxiety is like having a constant soundtrack of worry playing in your head. You might feel like you're always on edge, with sweaty palms, a racing heart, and a knot in your stomach. While a little bit of anxiety is expected (like before a big game or a first date), when it starts interfering with your daily life, that's when it becomes a problem.

Try these practical anxiety-busting techniques:

- **Controlled breathing:** Techniques like 4-7-8 breathing or box breathing can calm your nervous system:

   ○ **4-7-8 breathing:** Breathe in for four counts, hold for seven, and breathe out for eight. This is just one of many controlled breathing exercises. Despite being so simple to perform, this type of breathing has been found to reduce stress, increase alertness, and boost your immunity!
   ○ **Box breathing:** This works on counts of four and has a loop of four like a box. Breathe in for four counts, hold for four, breathe out for four, and hold for four. Then, do it again a few times.

- **Progressive muscle relaxation:** Tense and release muscle groups to reduce physical tension, starting with your toes and working up to your head. Literally, feel the stress leave your body.
- **Guided imagery:** Imagine a mini-vacation in your mind. Close your eyes and transport yourself to a peaceful oasis—maybe a sun-soaked beach or a serene mountaintop. Let the stress melt away as you immerse yourself in this calming mental landscape. Try free guided meditation apps or videos to enhance your experience. At the end of Chapter Thirteen, dive deeper with our Wellness Corner bonus resources.
- **Positive self-talk:** Replace negative thoughts with encouraging statements like, "I can handle this" or "This feeling will pass."
- **Gradual exposure to feared situations:** Face feared situations incrementally to build confidence.

For example, suppose big parties and social occasions fill you with anxiety. In that case, you might start by going out with one or two good friends, hosting a small get-together at your home, and perhaps visiting a friend for a small dinner party. Eventually, you can gradually attend more significant social occasions.
The idea is that instead of just jumping headfirst into a situation you fear, it is better to do so incrementally.

- **Keep an anxiety log:** Track anxiety triggers, symptoms, and coping strategies to identify patterns and track progress.

Depression

There are days when you're sad, especially if you got dumped, you failed a test, or something didn't go the way you'd hoped it would. Depression, however, is more than just feeling sad or having a bad day. It's a persistent feeling of hopelessness, worthlessness, and lack of interest in things you used to enjoy. When it hits you really hard, it can make even the simplest tasks feel impossible, like getting out of bed or taking a shower.

If you're struggling with depression, the most important thing to remember is that it's not your fault, and you're not alone. Anxiety and depression affect about one in five teens (Panchal, 2024), but the good news is that there is help available.

If you are struggling with depression:

- **Reach out:** Talk to a trusted adult or mental health professional.

- **Stay active:** Regular exercise can boost mood and energy levels. A jog or yoga stretch will flow blood and oxygen into your system. Exercise helps by releasing feel-good endorphins and taking your mind off your worries (Mayo Clinic, n.d.).
- **Maintain a healthy diet:** Proper nutrition supports mental health. Sugary treats and junk foods slow your metabolism and give you a sugar crash once they've worn off. Eating and drinking right can help you stabilize your blood sugar (glucose) levels and energize you throughout the day.
- **Express yourself:** Find healthy ways to share feelings, like talking or journaling. Bottling it up doesn't help.
- **Establish routines:** Regular schedules can provide structure and purpose. Include activities that will occupy your mind, such as building puzzles, arts and crafts, reading, and connecting with people and nature.
- **Seek professional health:** A mental health expert can provide tailored treatment strategies.

While lifestyle changes can help alleviate symptoms, professional help is often necessary. It's okay to ask for help. **Mental health challenges are common and treatable.** If you're struggling, don't hesitate to contact a counselor, therapist, or trusted adult. Your school or local community likely has resources available to support you.

Other Ways to Take Care of Your Mind

In addition to the strategies we've discussed, here are some powerful methods to further enhance your mental well-being.

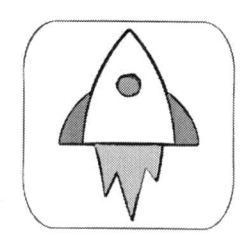

Acceptance and Commitment Therapy (ACT)

ACT is a unique approach to dealing with stress, anxiety, and depression. It allows "people to accept difficult thoughts, feelings, sensations, and internal experiences while guiding them to commit to values-based actions" (Glasofer, 2024). It is usually undertaken with the help of a therapist.

It teaches you to:

- Accept disturbing thoughts and feelings without fighting them. For example, instead of thinking, "I am a failure," you change it to "I am having a thought that I am a failure." It takes the focus off you and onto the thought.
- Discover and stay true to your core values. Staying happy and fulfilled even when everything doesn't work out as you hoped.
- Commit to actions that align with these values.

Stephen Hayes, the founder of ACT, illustrates its concepts using metaphors (pictures). See which one speaks to you the most.

- **Quicksand:** Struggling makes you sink deeper; accepting lets you float.
- **Thought train:** Watch negative thoughts pass by instead of boarding the train. You view each car on a train as a negative thought. Rather than getting on the train, you watch it go by. You're not looking "from" your thoughts but looking "at" them.
- **Leaves floating:** This is similar to the train. Imagine placing negative thoughts on leaves and watching them float away down a stream.

Mindfulness

Mindfulness is the practice of paying attention to the present moment without judgment. It can help reduce stress and improve focus. Try this five-senses exercise:

- Notice 5 things you can **see**
- Notice 4 things you can **feel**
- Notice 3 things you can **hear**
- Notice 2 things you can **smell**
- Notice 1 thing you can **taste**

Practice this regularly to develop a habit of present-moment awareness.

Your Mental Health Matters

Key takeaways:

- Your mental well-being is just as crucial as your physical health.
- Tools like CBT and ACT can help you manage mental health challenges.
- There's no shame in seeking help — reach out when you need support.
- Small, consistent steps can lead to significant improvements in your mental health.
- Taking care of your mental health is an ongoing journey.

But just before you nod and agree to look after your body and mind, there's one more part of your center, one more part that makes up you that is just as important.

As we move into the final chapter, we'll explore spiritual well-being for a truly holistic health approach. Your journey to becoming your best self is just beginning!

THIRTEEN

Nurturing Your Soul

> *You don't have a soul. You are a soul. You have a body.*
>
> C. S. Lewis

As we wrap up our journey of self-discovery, let's explore an often-overlooked aspect of personal growth: spirituality. Before you roll your eyes or picture incense and chanting monks, hear me out. Spirituality isn't always about organized religion or strict rules. It's about finding meaning in life and connecting your soul with something bigger than yourself.

Just like your body and mind, your soul needs TLC to thrive.

Now, I know spirituality can be a touchy subject. We all have different beliefs and experiences that shape our worldview. So, I'm about to share my personal take on spirituality. It has worked wonders for me, but it might not be your cup of tea. And that's totally okay! It is a journey that only you can discover and decide.

We live in a spiritual world where good and evil coexist. Recognizing this reality can profoundly impact our lives and choices. When we align ourselves with goodness — or God, for those who believe — we often find greater peace, purpose, and fulfillment.

The Power of Spiritual Health

Have you ever wondered why some people seem to radiate inner peace, even in tough times? The secret might lie in their spiritual health. Research has uncovered a fascinating link between spirituality and mental well-being. A 2015 survey found that people who actively participate in religious activities tend to experience more lasting happiness (Walsh, 2017). Let's unpack what spiritual health really means and how you can cultivate it, regardless of your beliefs.

Unraveling the Religion vs. Faith Mystery

Religion is like a map, while faith is the journey itself. Let's break it down:

- **Religion** often refers to an organized set of beliefs, complete with rituals, rules, and traditions. While religion can offer a solid framework for spiritual growth, following the rules doesn't automatically fulfill you spiritually.
- **Faith** is a more personal and intimate journey. It's about developing a deep, one-on-one connection with God beyond simply following rules. This personal relationship is built on trust and belief, allowing you to explore your spirituality in a way that feels authentic and meaningful.

Here's the kicker: you can have faith without being religious or follow religious practices without having genuine faith. The key is finding that balance that makes your soul sing.

The Hypocrisy Hurdle

Now, let's address the elephant in the room. Many of you might be rolling your eyes at the mention of religion. Why? Because you've seen people who talk a big spiritual game but don't always walk the walk. This hypocrisy can be incredibly frustrating and might make you want to ditch the whole spirituality thing altogether.

But here's some food for thought: Humans are flawed, messy, complicated creatures, regardless of our beliefs. We all struggle to live up to our ideals, whether religious or not. Someone stumbling on their spiritual path doesn't necessarily mean their beliefs are invalid. It's vital to separate human behavior from the underlying beliefs.

Finding Your Own Path

Interestingly, while many young people are turning away from traditional organized religion, studies show they're just as hungry for spirituality as previous generations. The fundamental human need for meaning, purpose, and connection to something greater hasn't changed – just how we pursue it. That's the soul speaking!

As you explore your soul, consider these approaches:

- **Question and explore:** Be bold and ask tough questions about life, meaning, and existence.
- **Look beyond labels:** Focus on belief systems' core teachings and values, not just the outward practices.
- **Find what resonates:** Pay attention to what gives you peace, purpose, or a sense of connection.
- **Practice compassion:** Remember, everyone's on their own spiritual journey – including you.
- **Seek authenticity:** Look for people and communities striving to live out their beliefs, even imperfectly.

Aligning with Good

We often face choices between good and evil, right and wrong. We frequently find greater peace and purpose when we align ourselves with "good" – or God.

Think of it like a chiropractic adjustment. When your spine is misaligned, you might experience various pains and ailments. Similarly, when we're spiritually "misaligned" – through actions like cheating, harboring resentment, or denying God's existence – we may feel inexplicable tension or distress.

The solution? Realign yourself with "good." This might involve:

- Owning up to mistakes
- Seeking and offering forgiveness
- Recommitting to your core values
- Reconnecting with your spiritual beliefs or practices

By doing this spiritual alignment, you might find that other areas of your life click into place more easily.

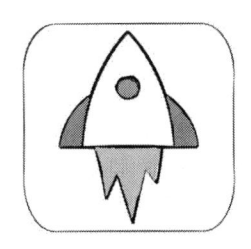

Practical Steps for Spiritual Alignment

The following tools can help you grow your spirituality, whatever your faith:

Gratitude

Start each day by acknowledging what you're grateful for. It could be something as simple as a cozy bed, a beautiful sunny day, or as significant as family, health, food, and shelter. This practice fosters a positive mindset and appreciation for life's blessings.

Try keeping a gratitude journal or creating a gratitude jar with notes about positive experiences. Research shows that regularly practicing gratitude can increase happiness, improve sleep, strengthen relationships, and boost overall health.

Meditation or Prayer

Spend a few minutes daily in quiet reflection through prayer or silent meditation. This time allows you to connect with God to seek wisdom and guidance.

If you're new to this practice, start with just a few minutes and consider using a guided app. Check out the Wellness Corner at the end of the chapter for bonus materials.

Inspiration

Begin your day with something uplifting—a devotional, podcast, or inspiring newsletter. This will set a positive tone and give you something to reflect on throughout the day.

Create a playlist of motivational speeches, poems, or songs to kickstart your mornings. You might also consider creating posters with positive affirmations like:

- "I am strong and brave."
- "I am beautiful, inside and out."
- "I have a purpose."

- "Every day is a fresh start."
- "Always stand up for your values."

Connection

Prioritize meaningful connections with others. This could be a heart-to-heart with a friend, a family dinner, or a call to mom and dad. These connections remind us we're part of something larger than ourselves.

Interestingly, many people find spiritual fulfillment in group activities as they provide a sense of community and belonging.

Giving

There is so much need out there! We get so wrapped up in our little world and our troubles that we sometimes forget how blessed we are. Giving to others is one of the most rewarding ways to nurture your soul.

This could mean a surprise visit to your grandparents or the elderly in your life, volunteering or giving to a local charity, helping a friend with a project, or simply offering a listening ear or a kind word. You'll gain a sense of purpose and perspective by making a positive difference in someone else's life.

Creative Expression and Movement

Use art, music, or writing to explore your feelings. Also, regular physical activity isn't just good for your body and mind — it's great for your soul. Whether it's a nature walk, a gym session, or playing paddle, find a form of movement that energizes and grounds you.

Enjoyment

Embracing joy and humor can profoundly impact your well-being, creating a sense of lightness and happiness that resonates deep within your soul.

During all your activities and responsibilities, don't forget to make time for the things that bring you joy—whether it's laughing out loud, playing video games, scrolling through memes, watching cat videos (let's be honest, those are pretty funny), or just goofing around with friends. Whatever it is, don't deny it. Find some time for enjoyment, even if it's mindless.

Appreciation

Take time to appreciate the people, places, and experiences that make your life rich and meaningful. Write thank-you notes, share compliments, do acts of kindness, or simply pause to savor life's beauty. By cultivating a sense of appreciation, you train your mind to focus on the good and attract more of it into your life.

Reflection

End each day with a few minutes of reflection. Ponder life's big questions. Consider what went well, what you learned, and what you're grateful for. This helps process the day's events and set intentions for tomorrow. Every day is an opportunity to start again!

Remember, spiritual growth is a personal journey. What works for one person may not work for another. Finding practices that resonate with you helps you feel connected to something larger than yourself and find peace. Remain open, curious, and committed to your growth.

Wellness Corner

To help you integrate the lessons learned into your daily life, here are some activities, prompts, and action items to enhance your holistic well-being:

Journal Prompts

- What does "balance" mean to you regarding mind, body, and soul?
- Describe a moment when you felt completely at peace. What contributed to that feeling?
- If you could ask God one question, what would it be?
- Recall a kindness that touched your heart deeply. How did it change you?
- What food choices did you make today? How did they affect your energy?
- How many hours did you sleep today? Was it quality sleep?
- How did you exercise your body today?
- Did I laugh out loud today?

Interactive Activities

- **30-Day Wellness Challenge:** Create a calendar with daily tasks focusing on physical, mental, and spiritual health.
- **Gratitude Jar:** Write down one thing you're grateful for daily and add it to a jar.

Action Items

- Write a letter to your future self, describing the person you aspire to become.
- Create a weekly meal plan that nourishes your body and mind.
- Establish a consistent sleep routine and track its effects on your mood and energy.
- Try a new form of exercise or movement each week for a month.
- Engage in one act of kindness each day for a week.
- Start a prayer or meditation practice with just 5 minutes daily.
- Connect with nature by spending time outdoors daily, even just a few minutes.
- Reach out to a friend or family member for a meaningful conversation about life and purpose.

Expand Your Wellness Corner

Ready for more? Scan the QR code below to access bonus resources, including videos, recommended tools, apps, and extra body, mind, and soul tips. Check back often for updates and fresh content.

Balancing Mind, Body, and Soul

Actual well-being comes from nurturing all aspects of ourselves—mind, body, and soul. When these are in harmony, we're better equipped to handle life's challenges and find joy in our experiences.

Remember, balance doesn't mean perfection. It's about making consistent efforts in each area and adjusting as needed.

You've made it to the end of this incredible journey of self-discovery and growth. You've completed the compass. Every point is in place, and that needle looks sharp and accurate, pointing you in the right direction.

Inspire Others to Persevere

As you close the last pages of this book, I hope you are excited about trying out the many strategies and tips I have shared—from working out your ideal course or profession to making your first investments and surrounding yourself with a supportive community. I have highlighted the importance of maintaining a growth mindset throughout your journey of self-discovery.

Still, there is a second tool I hope you always take with you: **perseverance**. Albert Einstein once said he wasn't so bright; he just "stayed with problems longer." This is the essence of success—whether at school, in your social life, or alone. I hope that this book has inspired you to trust your internal compass, even if, now and again, you feel a little lost. You, too, can lead the way for someone else, and a worthwhile place to start is by sharing your opinion of this book with others. And if you are inspired, include a photo or video showcasing how you interacted with this book. Your visual story could be the spark someone else needs to begin their journey of self-discovery.

TAKE A MOMENT TO SHARE YOUR THOUGHTS!

Wishing you many beautiful years of discovery, joy, and fulfillment in the years ahead. Because young adulthood is so mysterious, it is also one of life's most extraordinary adventures.

Angela Abraham

SCAN ME

It's a Wrap!

This is it! Can you believe it? You really put in some great work; congratulations!

Throughout this book, we've explored what it truly means to thrive. You've gained powerful tools and strategies to discover your unique strengths and passions, hone your skills, craft an unstoppable mindset, strengthen your circle of trust, master your money, and take care of your holistic well-being.

But here's the real magic: you've learned that authentic fulfillment comes from within. It's about understanding, crystal clear, who you are, what sets your soul on fire, and how you want to show up. When you're grounded in that unshakable sense of self, you become the master of your own destiny. No challenge is too big; no setback can keep you down for long. You have everything you need to create a life overflowing with purpose, passion, and joy.

As we wrap up our epic adventure together, I want to leave you with a few key takeaways:

- **Balance is key.** Strive for equilibrium in your emotions, relationships, finances, and life choices. Find the sweet spot between hard work and enjoyment, between having fun and being responsible.
- **Every decision counts.** Remember that each choice you make, no matter how small, brings you closer to or further from your goals and the person you want to become. Choose wisely and intentionally.
- **Your uniqueness is your superpower.** Embrace what makes you different and use it to blaze your own trail.
- **Challenges are growth opportunities.** When life throws you curveballs, remember it's a chance to level up and come back stronger than ever.
- **Your vibe attracts your tribe.** Surround yourself with people who lift you up, inspire you to be your best self, and make you laugh until your face hurts.
- **You are the CEO of your own life.** Take ownership of your choices, learn from your mistakes, and keep pushing toward your dreams.
- **Investing in yourself is the best investment you'll ever make.** Prioritize your personal growth, take risks, and never stop learning.

Here's my last challenge: pick one insight or lesson from this book that resonated with you and put it into action today. Share it with a friend, write it on a Post-it Note, or make it your phone background. And tomorrow, do it again. Small steps, taken consistently, lead to massive transformations over time.

Remember, this isn't the end of your journey—it's just the beginning. Keep exploring, keep growing, and keep shining your unique light. The world needs your magic now more than ever.

And whenever you need a reminder of how incredible you are, just flip back through these pages. Let the words be a compass guiding you back to your own inner wisdom and strength. Because the truth is, you've had the power within you all along. This book simply helped you unlock it.

So go forth and conquer, my friend! Embrace unexpected moments, dance in the rain, and never forget how wildly capable you are. The best is yet to come, and I can't wait to see all the fantastic places your journey takes you.

Here's to your amazing next chapter—let's make it legendary!

References

Abrams, Zara. "The Science of Why Friendships Keep Us Healthy." American Psychological Association. June 1, 2023.

Ackerman, Courtney E. "Big Five Personality Traits: The OCEAN Model Explained." Positive Psychology. April 25, 2024.

Amen Clinics. "Healthy vs. Unhealthy Brain SPECT Images." Accessed July 8, 2024. https://www.amenclinics.com/gallery/healthy-vs-unhealthy-brain-spect-images/.

Bieber, Christy. "Revealing Divorce Statistics in 2024." Forbes. May 30, 2024.

Bloom, Sahil. "Sahil Bloom." Accessed May 8, 2024. https://www.sahilbloom.com/.

Bradberry, Travis, and Jean Greaves. *Emotional Intelligence 2.0.* San Diego, CA: TalentSmart, 2009.

Brown, Brené. *Dare to Lead: Brave Work. Tough Conversations. Whole Hearts.* New York: Random House, 2018.

Burchard, Brendon. *High Performance Habits: How Extraordinary People Become That Way.* Carlsbad, CA: Hay House, Inc., 2017.

Cam. "The Feynman Technique." University of Colorado Boulder. August 7, 2020.

Carnegie, Dale. *How to Win Friends AND Influence People.* New York: Simon & Schuster, 2013.

Carson, Ben. *You Have a Brain: A Teen's Guide to T.H.I.N.K. B.I.G.* Grand Rapids, MI: Zondervan, 2015.

Cherry, Kendra. "What Is Procrastination?" Verywell Mind. November 14, 2022.

Cherry, Kendra. "How Multitasking Affects Productivity and Brain Health." Verywell Mind. March 1, 2023.

Clear, James. *Atomic Habits: An Easy & Proven Way to Build Good Habits & Break Bad Ones.* New York: Avery, 2018.

Clear, James. "The Ivy Lee Method: The Daily Routine Experts Recommend for Peak Productivity." James Clear. Accessed June 10, 2024. https://jamesclear.com/ivy-lee.

Dalio, Ray. *Principles: Life and Work.* New York: Simon & Schuster, 2017.

Duke, Annie. *Thinking in Bets: Making Smarter Decisions When You Don't Have All the Facts.* New York: Portfolio/Penguin, 2018

Dweck, Carol S. *Mindset: The New Psychology of Success.* New York: Random House, 2006.

Fernando, Jason. "Financial Literacy: What It Is, and Why It Is So Important to Teach Kids." Investopedia. April 12, 2024 (1). https://www.investopedia.com/terms/f/financial-literacy.asp.

Fleming, LaKeisha. "Character and Personality Are Actually Two Different Things—Here's Why." Verywell Mind. August 21, 2023.

Gartner. "Gartner HR Research Finds 58% of the Workforce Will Need New Skill Sets to Do Their Jobs Successfully." Accessed June 29, 2024. https://www.gartner.com/en/newsroom/press-releases/2021-02-03-gartner-hr-research-finds-fifty-eight-percent-of-the-workforce-will-need-new-skill-sets-to-do-their-jobs-successfully.

Glasofer, Deborah R. "What Is Acceptance and Commitment Therapy (ACT)?" Verywell Mind. January 16, 2024.

Goldberg, Lewis R. "An Alternative 'Description of Personality': The Big-Five Factor Structure." *Journal of Personality and Social Psychology*, 59, no. 6 (1990): 1216–1229.

Gumbel, Nicky, and Pippa Gumbel. *The Bible*, Classic Version. Accessed 2024. Bible App.

Hartney, Elizabeth. "10 Cognitive Distortions That Can Cause Negative Thinking." Verywell Mind. November 8, 2023.

Kiyosaki, Robert T. *Rich Dad Poor Dad: What the Rich Teach Their Kids About Money That the Poor and Middle Class Do Not!.* Scottsdale, AZ: Plata Publishing, 2011.

194 • References

Lui, Calvin. "Teen Obesity." Sutter Health. July, 2019.

Manrique, Esteban. "The Importance of Soft Skills." LinkedIn. March 11, 2024.

Martin, Sharon. "7 Types of Boundaries." PsychCentral. April 23,2020.

Mass General Brigham McLean. "The Social Dilemma: Social Media and Your Mental Health." Accessed June 7, 2024. https://www.mcleanhospital.org/essential/it-or-not-social-medias-affecting-your-mental-health

Mayo Clinic Staff. "Depression and Anxiety: Exercise Eases Symptoms." Accessed June 12, 2024. https://www.mayoclinic.org/diseases-conditions/depression/in-depth/depression-and-exercise/art-20046495.

McGinnis, Alan Loy. *The Friendship Factor: How to Get Closer to the People You Care for.* Minneapolis, MN: Augsburg Publishing House, 1979.

Mehrabian, Albert. *Silent Messages.* Belmont, CA: Wadsworth Publishing Company, 1981.

Mercer. "Global Talent Trends 2021 Report: Win with Empathy." New York: Mercer LLC, 2021.

National Center for Drug Abuse Statistics. "Drug Use Among Youth: Facts & Statistics." Accessed June 9, 2024. https://drugabusestatistics.org/teen-drug-use/.

National Institute on Alcohol Abuse and Alcoholism. "Get the Facts about Underage Drinking." February, 2024.

Nemours TeensHealth. "When Being Overweight Is a Health Problem." April, 2022.

Newberry, Tommy. *The 4:8 Principle: The Secret to a Joy-Filled Life.* Carol Stream, IL: Tyndale House Publishers, 2007.

Our World in Data. "Who Americans Spend Their Time With, Age by Age." Accessed June 7, 2024. https://ourworldindata.org/grapher/time-spent-with-relationships-by-age-us.

Panchal, Nirmita. "Recent Trends in Mental Health and Substance Use Concerns among Adolescents." KFF. February 6, 2024.

Peterson, Jordan B. *12 Rules for Life: An Antidote to Chaos.* Toronto: Random House Canada, 2018.

Robson, David. "Why Alcohol Is So Damaging for Young Adults' Brains." BBC. March 1, 2024.

Satterfield, Jason. *Cognitive Behavioral Therapy: Techniques for Retraining Your Brain.* The Great Courses, 2015.

Shatz, Itamar. "Procrastination Statistics: Interesting and Useful Statistics about Procrastination." Solving Procrastination. Accessed June 12, 2024. https://solvingprocrastination.com/procrastination-statistics/.

Siler, Adiah. "This Is What Phone Addiction Looks Like for Teens and How Parents Can Help." Parents. January 12, 2024.

Simplilearn. "12 Analytical Skills Necessary for a Successful Career in Data Science." April 30, 2024.

Six Seconds. "Plutchik's Wheel of Emotions: Exploring the Emotion Wheel." Accessed Jun 7, 2024. https://www.6seconds.org/2022/03/13/plutchik-wheel-emotions/.

Springer, Bill. "Kids Who Travel Do Better in School." Forbes. January 31, 2019.

The University of Queensland. "How Many Career Changes in a Lifetime?" June 19, 2023.

Therapist Aid. "Personal Values Worksheet." Accessed June 11, 2024. https://www.therapistaid.com/worksheets/personal-values-circles.

Townsend, John. *Boundaries for Teens: When to Say Yes, How to Say No.* Grand Rapids, MI: Zondervan, 2006.

U.S. Securities and Exchange Commission. "Compound Interest Calculator." Investor.gov. Accessed June 4, 2024. https://www.investor.gov/financial-tools-calculators/calculators/compound-interest-calculator.

US Bureau of Labor Statistics. "Education Pays." Accessed June 3, 2024. https://www.bls.gov/emp/chart-unemployment-earnings-education.htm.

University of Rochester Medical Center. "5-4-3-2-1 Coping Technique for Anxiety."

Accessed June 13, 2024. https://www.urmc.rochester.edu/behavioral-health-partners/bhp-blog/april-2018/5-4-3-2-1-coping-technique-for-anxiety.aspx

Villas-Boas, Ana García. "Positivity Is Not Magic. It's Science." IE Insights. February 1, 2022.

Vinay. "The Importance of an Internship: 5 Reasons Why Internships Are Critical." Capital Placement. May 29, 2020.

Walsh, Bryan. "Does Spirituality Make You Happy?" Time. August 7, 2017.

Welding, Lyss. "Average Student Loan Debt: 2024 Statistics." Best Colleges. May 30, 2024.

Wenk, Gary. "Why Do Teenagers Feel Immortal?" Psychology Today. August 23, 2010.

White, Alexandria. "73% of Americans Rank Their Finances as the No. 1 Stress in Life, According to New Capital One CreditWise Survey." CNBC. May 20, 2024.

White-Gibson, Zuri. "Resilience in Teens: Customizing your Mental Toolkit." PsychCentral. June 21, 2022.

World Economic Forum. "Future of Jobs Report 2023." Accessed June 29, 2024. https://www.weforum.org/reports/the-future-of-jobs-report-2023/.

Yahoo Finance. "SPDR S&P 500 ETF Trust (SPY) Historical Data." Accessed June 4, 2024. https://finance.yahoo.com/quote/SPY/history/.